LOVE until DEATH

The twisted true story of killer conman
Alexandre Despallières

BY CHRIS HUTCHINS

EBURY
SPOTLIGHT

1

Ebury Spotlight, an imprint of Ebury Publishing
20 Vauxhall Bridge Road
London SW1V 2SA

Ebury Spotlight is part of the Penguin Random House group of companies
whose addresses can be found at global.penguinrandomhouse.com

Penguin
Random House
UK

First published by Ebury Spotlight in 2024

www.penguin.co.uk

A CIP catalogue record for this book is available from the British Library

ISBN 9781529903751

Typeset in 11/17pt Bembo Book MT Pro by Jouve (UK), Milton Keynes
Printed and bound in Great Britain by Clays Ltd, Elcograf S.p.A.

The authorised representative in the EEA is Penguin Random House Ireland,
Morrison Chambers, 32 Nassau Street, Dublin D02 YH68

Penguin Random House is committed to a sustainable future
for our business, our readers and our planet. This book is made
from Forest Stewardship Council® certified paper.

*I dedicate this book to Billy Gaff, John Reid, Chris Laffaille and
my wife, Gerri Hutchins, who did so much to make it happen,
and of course to the memory of Peter Ikin.*

*So many others contributed information which brought this
tangled story to life. Most of them are named in these pages.*

AUTHOR'S NOTE

This book is the product of more than 200 interviews with people who crossed paths with the enigmatic Alexandre Despallières, as well as those who knew and loved the late Peter Ikin.

All facts are taken from the author's research, police reports and court transcripts, and with the cooperation of the French Brigade Criminelle.

It should also be noted that many documents from the dossier used to compile this authoritative account of events were provided to me with permission to publish by Despallières himself, including a number of the photographs.

Thanks to friends who kindly passed on his emails, many of the words contained herein are also from Ikin himself.

TABLE OF CONTENTS

PROLOGUE

CHRISTMAS 2010

Outside, a light falling of snow dusts the fir trees at the end of the garden. From somewhere further down the road comes the sound of carols and across the way the happy noise of laughter emerges from a crowd of early revellers. On top of the hill, I can see the tower of St Matthias Church brightly illuminated – an extravagance allowed just once a year, at Christmastime.

I look down once more at the words neatly written on the single sheet of lined A4 paper in my hand. It is a letter from my newest correspondent:

> My dear friend Chris,
>
> It is my turn to wish you a Merry Christmas and a Happy New Year. May it bring health, love and happiness to you and your family.
>
> Your friend,
> Alex

My 'friend' is a Frenchman named Alexandre Despallières – a man who, up to this point, I have never met. The letter has been written from his cell in a bleak Paris prison.

So who is Alex? Is he the particularly gifted man whose IT business interests have netted him billions of dollars? A close friend of Carlos Slim and the Sultan of Brunei, whose generosity and charm has beguiled the world's elite?

Or is he the cold-blooded killer accused by the French police of poisoning his lover, Peter Ikin, just a matter of days after they entered a civil union? A ruthless but brilliant conman who made millions by creating a fictitious persona and ingratiating his way into the lives of the rich and famous?

Perhaps only time would tell.

Alexandre Despallières began writing to me once he learned from a mutual contact that I had set out to uncover the truth about him, and to chronicle the extraordinary chain of events that led to his incarceration. His letters are full of convincing phrases and expressions of good intent. But then those who became his friends – or were they victims? – would say the same of his words and actions towards them during this incredible tale.

The letter in my hand is one of dozens I will receive from him in the months and years ahead, many of them containing good wishes to me and my wife urging us to take care of our health. He would seek my advice on all manner of subjects, including whether he should give television interviews once freed from prison.

Though no more than a passing acquaintance of the late Peter Ikin, I was close to several of his friends and, as a result, would be drawn into this story. I know I will have to meet Despallières, to talk at length to those who love and hate him in equal measure, to listen to lurid accusations and impossible explanations. It's a journey I will at times come to regret.

But it's Christmas, and at least I am not the one having to spend it in a prison cell. How will it all end for him? I wonder, as the carol singers reach my front door . . .

CHAPTER 1
A DARK SILENCE

I had stood on this platform of St Pancras Station on numerous occasions in the past, mostly setting off from London for happy events such as holidays, or journeying to see a loved one. This chilly April morning in 2011 was different. As families with noisy children waited alongside me to board the Eurostar to Paris, I viewed my journey with some trepidation – with good reason. I was on my way to spend time interviewing a man whom I had met briefly a month earlier for the first time, but who had been writing to me for two years. Even the magnificence of the Gothic architecture of this London landmark could not distract me from my unease about my mission. Precisely why was I going to Paris? What was I going to learn there? I wasn't sure. What I did know was that Alexandre Despallières had a story to tell, and I was anxious to hear it.

Three years earlier, Despallières had lost his partner, Peter Ikin, in tragic circumstances just 33 days after they had entered into a civil partnership in London. Ikin had been a much-loved and respected figure on the international music scene, adored by all and none more so than his 'beloved Alex'.

As the train sped through the Channel Tunnel and the attendant served me a much-needed Bloody Mary, I thought about Peter Ikin. I hadn't known him well – we'd had dinner on a couple of occasions, but he'd been extremely close to two good friends of mine, Billy Gaff and John Reid, who'd both turned artists they'd managed into global superstars: in Gaff's case it was Rod Stewart and in Reid's Elton John.

Ikin had taken a tumble in a hotel in Paris and his death, decreed the coroner, was the result of heart failure. He was in his sixties, overweight thanks to his healthy appetite, and not particularly fit, so although people were shocked at his sudden departure, they were not that surprised. The man I was about to talk to was heavily invested in that version of events.

In the taxi that ferried me from the Gare du Nord I went over in my mind the events that had led me to this journey.

· · ·

As Billy Gaff inserted the key in the lock of his hotel room door, his mobile phone began to ring. He pushed the door open and stepped into his suite, a palatial set of rooms in the tower of Miami's Four Seasons Hotel. He liked luxury and was always discerning in his choice of hotel. This one suited him perfectly.

He was in high spirits. After spending a few days visiting close friends in New York he had flown into Miami on this November day in 2008 to catch a connecting flight to the South

American city of Quito, where he was to be joined by his closest friend of all, Peter Ikin.

The adventurous pair were due to embark on a cruise to the Galapagos Islands, 'a step back into history' as Ikin had described it when they'd made the booking almost two years earlier. As ever, they had booked the owner's suite, for nothing but the best would do for these two music industry moguls. Between them they had made many millions – Gaff in managing artists including Rod Stewart, the American rock star John Cougar Mellencamp, and running his own record label and music publishing interests; Ikin as a senior executive with Warner Music, a division of what was to become AOL Time Warner, the world's second-largest entertainment conglomerate.

The last time the two men had been together was when they'd crossed the Atlantic aboard the *Queen Mary*: on a visit to one of the ship's bars, Ikin had discovered Rod Stewart was there. The singer expressed surprise but that was nothing compared to his reaction when Ikin produced Gaff, whom he had not seen since they'd parted company following an acrimonious High Court action to dissolve their business relationship. Happily, the unscheduled reunion went off without a hitch.

Now, no longer tied to their highly lucrative but exacting charges, Gaff and Ikin were free to roam the world first-class, sleeping in opulent hotel suites and indulging their tastes for good food and fine wine. Although their homes were continents apart – Irishman Gaff living in Bangkok with a second home on the French Riviera and a third in South Wales, and Ikin dividing his time between London and his native Sydney – the two had been close friends for over 30 years and saw each other regularly.

Buoyed by the prospect of seeing his friend in just a few hours, Gaff answered the call and walked to the window, taking in the view across the clear waters of Biscayne Bay. 'Is the weather there as glorious as it is here?' he asked, immediately recognising the voice on the other end of the line.

The caller was David Robinson, a long-time friend of Ikin, and he was phoning from his home in Bangkok, although the news he had to convey had come from Ikin's former secretary Anne Marie Nicol in London, and she had received it from Paris. 'Billy, I have some dreadful news – Peter is dead.'

'No, don't be silly,' was Gaff's admonishing response. 'He's coming here tomorrow; we are meeting up in Ecuador for a cruise. You've made a mistake. You must mean Alex Despallières: we've been expecting him to die for a long time. How sad, but inevitable in view of his poor health condition.'

'No, Billy, no mistake. Peter is dead. He died in Paris, in a hotel. Apparently, he had a heart attack and fell down some stairs. He's gone, Billy. We've lost him.'

A dark silence fell as Gaff took in the news. For once he was lost for words. He felt the blood drain from his face as he realised there was no mistake: 'I felt numb from head to foot,' he would later say. From the comfort of his lounger just minutes earlier, he had been content to watch other guests cavort beside the hotel pool in the dazzling sunlight. Everything in his life had seemed to be exactly as he wanted it. Now, suddenly, his world was shattered. Tears filled his eyes as memories of his dear friend tumbled through his mind while he struggled to accept the awful news he had just received.

But perhaps, just perhaps, David Robinson had got it wrong. After all, Alex was the one who was dying . . .

CHAPTER 2

AN UNEXPECTED ARRIVAL

Alexandre Renaud Marcel Despallières turned up at the door of Peter Ikin's Sydney apartment unannounced. It was April 2008 and although the two men had been lovers more than two decades earlier, they had seen each other only occasionally since, and not at all in recent times.

'How are you, Peter? May I come in?'

Ikin was so surprised by the arrival of his unexpected visitor that he kept him standing in the doorway. Unable to find the right words, he finally gestured his guest inside.

Approaching his 62nd birthday, the older man's girth was spreading and, now retired, he was paying less attention to his physical appearance than he had done previously. Some 20 years his junior, Despallières, by contrast, had lost none of the handsome features his former lover remembered, and he had retained the same slim physique. Indeed, as Ikin was to say later, Despallières looked more attractive than ever.

'Still the same old Peter,' said the new arrival, casting his eyes over the immaculate interior of the Kincoppal apartment – a fashionable building once home to Rupert Murdoch and David Bowie. Magazines were all lined up, tops of the covers each exactly an inch below the one above it. Ikin had a formidable reputation for being meticulous. If the pencil on his desk was not at a right angle to the eraser beside it, he was in turmoil, rearranging everything until it fitted the required pattern. Every garment in his wardrobe was wrapped in polythene covers and a Post-it note would serve as a reminder of when he'd last worn it – not that he needed much reminding about anything.

Ikin still said nothing. He was staring at the man he had once called his 'beloved Alex' and thinking back to their first meeting in the summer of 1988, when Despallières had been 19 years old. At that time Ikin had been one of the great power brokers of the international record business, immensely popular with both his peers and the star names he worked alongside. A hugely inquisitive, larger-than-life character, he floated in and out of their lives, never making waves, never making enemies. He loved to gossip and was privy to more secrets than most. As Sir Elton John was to put it: 'Peter was a fabulous person . . . It is such a tragedy that he has been taken from us.' Indeed, Elton liked him so much that when Ikin had co-founded Australia's annual music awards, the ARIAs, the star had agreed to host the show.

In addition to his good looks, Alexandre Despallières was not only charming but also highly intelligent, from a respectable middle-class Parisian family. Ikin had always believed that his friend was destined for great things. Nothing, he said, would ever stand in Alexandre's way.

They'd first met in San Francisco in 1988. It was a city famous for having a high-profile gay population and was thrust into the limelight as the world grappled with an AIDS epidemic that had emerged earlier that decade. Trials of the new drug AZT were already promising, although they would not have known that at the time. Only one of the pair would escape the AIDS epidemic unscathed.

Both men were in the city for a Warner convention – Ikin was a senior executive of the international conglomerate, having risen rapidly through the ranks to his lofty position, largely due to his remarkable ability to befriend the stars, whose interests he guarded as closely as his employers'. Rod Stewart and Elton John (the latter dubbed him Iris: he often gave female names to men he was fond of) were just two of the global hit-makers who were happy to call him their friend. The pair's respective managers, Billy Gaff and John Reid, also grew close to him, as later did Madonna and a host of others at the top of their tree.

Despallières's reason for being there was less clear. He had been accredited to the convention as a lighting assistant – a modest job description for a man who had recently come within touching distance of stardom in his native France with the release of a promising recording of a song he'd written himself called 'L'Amour à mort' ('Love Until Death'). Claude Nobs, who was there in his capacity as promoter of the Montreux Jazz Festival had taken him under his wing after they'd apparently met through a telephone dating service. It was Nobs who introduced him to Ikin. 'The next thing I knew Peter and Alex were an item,' says Billy Gaff. 'Not long afterwards Peter came for champagne at the Helmsley Palace Hotel in New York where I was staying with my partner, Steve Andrews, and he had Alex with him. He was clearly besotted.'

Both men, however, had busy lives and friends testify that although they were clearly fond of each other, their meetings were intermittent and in far-flung corners of the world. However, several years after he had entertained them with champagne in New York, Gaff took a call from Ikin in his native Dublin. 'He said he would like to come and stay with me for a few days and asked if he could bring Alex with him. "What, Alex from New York?"' came Gaff's response, with a certain amount of incredulity, surprised to hear his friend mention the name after so long.

Gaff readily agreed to the request once he heard Ikin's reason for making it: 'He told me that Alex wanted to talk to my Steve because he was HIV positive.' Steve also had HIV and would sadly die of AIDS in 1995. Ikin went on to explain that Alex had discovered he had HIV when he was aged 16, and that he'd contracted it from a contaminated needle. While it might have seemed that unprotected sex was a more likely cause, Gaff didn't bat an eyelid, 'because at that time so many of the young men I knew were either dead or dying from the illness – three of them died in my house – so I had become immune to such announcements'.

The duo duly arrived in Ireland and Gaff's sister, Miriam, quickly formed a bond with the young Alex. 'She decided that he was the nicest, kindest, most charming man she had ever met. And Miriam was a pretty good judge of character by anyone's standards.' As she later told me: 'Billy had never had such a charming guest. Alex would go to the kitchen after we had had a meal and wash the dishes. It was all any of the others could do to pour themselves another glass of champagne.'

After their visit to Dublin, the couple's romance seemed to dwindle. Ikin, a workaholic living on the other side of the world, fell out of touch with his young lover and, in the years that followed, he rarely spoke of his old flame. As Gaff relates, 'The only time Alex's name was mentioned after that was a few years ago when I was on my annual trip to Sydney. For some reason I went to Peter's room which I would never normally do, and I noticed that one of the several photographs on his bedside table was of a very handsome man. "Peter," I asked, "who is that gorgeous young man?" And he said, "That's Alex." I said I would never have recognised him because he looked so much better than I remembered him and Peter said, "Yes, he's matured well." I was just surprised that he had survived so long in view of his condition. Peter never did say why they had drifted apart but that's the way affairs often go.'

. . .

So here, all those years on, in the drawing room of Peter Ikin's apartment stood the kind, charming, disarmingly handsome man with whom Ikin – now eight years into his cosseted retirement – had once appeared so besotted.

Ikin asked the only question he could think of at that moment: 'Alex, it's wonderful to see you again after all this time, but what are you doing in Sydney?'

Diverting his gaze from the magnificent view across the harbour, the exceedingly polite Frenchman asked if they might sit down. He had, he said, a lot to relay.

Ikin listened in amazement as the softly spoken Despallières began to recount what had happened in the years since they had last met. First, he said, he had to answer Ikin's question about what he was doing in the city. He had travelled there from America, where he now lived, to attend an IT industry convention as its keynote speaker: fortune had smiled on him so kindly that his own IT business had grown extensively, and he was now extremely wealthy. As a result, he had many interesting new friends, one of whom was the grandson of one of the world's richest men, Carlos Slim. A self-made billionaire from Mexico, Slim was at the time jostling for the top spot with computer king Bill Gates and businessman Warren Buffett. Through that connection, Despallières was currently involved in negotiations to sell Slim his business, a deal that was going to net him billions of dollars. To prove his claims, he brandished a photograph of Slim's grandson, the dealmaker.

Despallières did not need the money for he was already worth tens of millions, but he had an urgent reason for wanting to unload the company which, he said, he would come to. First he had to tell his friend of yesteryear just how well he had done: his home was now a Californian mansion on Doheny Drive in Beverly Hills, and he also had a luxurious house in the centre of Paris. Although he was embarrassed to admit it, the jewel in his property crown was a six-bedroom New York apartment at the city's most prestigious address, 15 Central Park West, where he was on nodding terms with such illustrious neighbours as Ikin's friends Madonna, Denzel Washington and Sting.

Ikin was staggered. He wanted to make coffee but could not bring himself to get up from his seat. Born into a financially comfortable family himself, Ikin had retired in 2000 after a long stint as London-based Warner Music International senior vice president of international marketing and artist development, a post he had held since 1991. His earlier career included being managing director of the US repertoire division of Warner Music Australia from 1987 to 1991, and prior to that he was with EMI Australia. He had accrued what he considered a fortune – but that was millions, not billions. His emotions were mixed – part admiration for what his friend had achieved, part envy.

Why, he now wanted to know, was Alex about to sell up? Why not keep going until he reached the stage where he could buy out Carlos Slim rather than the other way around?

Those were the crunch questions and the answer they elicited was shattering. 'Peter, I am dying,' Despallières began. 'You know that I have been HIV positive for years. Well, now I have AIDS. I have so little time left – the doctors say six months at the most.'

Ikin was speechless. First some of the greatest news he had ever received, now the worst. He had often thought of Despallières, reflected on their times together, even dug out old photographs of them together, taken almost two decades earlier. His eyes welled up, but Despallières had yet another dramatic announcement to make, finally coming to the point of his visit. He explained that under French law his two brothers, Marc and Jean-Michel, would inherit much of his fortune. 'I don't want that to happen, Peter. They are evil men. They did terrible things to me. I want you to have it, to have it all.'

Ikin gulped. Only minutes earlier he had heard of the incredible fortune his former lover had amassed. Now was it really to be all his? Was he dreaming? Was Alexandre Despallières really here, sat in front of him, on the verge of death and offering him the earth? A final question crossed his mind: what was wanted in return?

The answer came even before he could pose the question: Despallières leaned forward, placed his hand on the older man's knee and, almost in a whisper, began, 'Peter, marry me. It's what I have always wanted and in your heart of hearts, I believe it's what you wanted too. I will die happy, and you will be rich beyond your dreams. Once we have entered a civil union you will be sole heir to everything I have. My brothers will not be able to touch it. We must do it soon, there is so little time.'

For his stay in Sydney, Despallières had spurned the five-star hotel where the IT convention he was speaking at was being held and had booked himself into a bijou hostelry where he would not be pestered by those anxious to be seen in the company of a man who had overtaken them all in the achievement stakes. Staying with him was his personal assistant, an amiable young Frenchman called Jérémy Bilien, 14 years younger than Despallières and very much in his shadow.

Stunned by what he had just been told, all Ikin could think to do was to insist that the pair move into his apartment. While Despallières went to collect his belongings and his assistant, Ikin busied himself retrieving photographs of Despallières and himself from a locked drawer and placing them on tables around the drawing room: 'To make my French beau feel at home,' as he was to tell Gaff, one man who was to become privy to the secret of their reunion.

The arrival of guests was not without an element of discomfort for Ikin, however. A lifelong bachelor with strict household rules, he had to stifle annoyance at some aspects of sharing his home with two men who did not conform to his high standards. On top of that, Despallières smoked 60 cigarettes a day, creating an unwelcome fog. However, Ikin decided against making a fuss. It was not the time to ask Despallières to give up such a vice.

What Despallières lacked in matters of domestic cleanliness, he more than made up for with fascinating tales in their long, late-night discussions about all he had achieved along the road to the dizzying heights of his career. A television buff himself, Ikin was particularly interested to learn that he had written several episodes of the highly acclaimed television series *Boston*

Legal, for a man who he said had become a close friend, the show's creator, David E. Kelley. A winner of five Emmys, *Boston Legal* was from the same stable as *L.A. Law* and starred William Shatner and Candice Bergen, among others. What Ikin didn't know was that Kelley was notorious for neither needing nor wanting co-writers on projects. Later there was talk of Despallières's collaboration on *House*, the popular medical drama starring Hugh Laurie.

Openness, however, ended at the door of the apartment the trio now occupied. Ikin regarded Sydney's close-knit community as a bitchy enclave of gossips who would dine off the story of what was now happening in his life for years to come. Despallières and all that his arrival entailed had, he decreed, to remain a secret – a situation that was to dog their relationship in the months ahead.

It was not until some six weeks later, at the end of May, that he would finally break the news to his closest friend and confidant, Billy Gaff, in an email. 'We are an item and we are going to try and share our lives,' he wrote. 'Alex openly tells people he is my boyfriend – many tears [have been] shed on both sides but we have always shared a very special bond based on love and trust . . . He says that after 20 years he is ready and waiting no longer, as he has only ever loved me.'

At that point, Ikin introduced a note of doubt about what his response should be: 'Did I want to share my life with him as he does his with me? It was like a proposal so I had to say yes – how could I say no?'

Despallières's wish that the pair of them should live in New York was not going to be fulfilled, though Ikin told Gaff that he was happy to arrange a compromise and had rearranged his schedule for the weeks ahead so that he could travel to New York early the following month 'to see my new residence at Central Park West'.

In New York, Ikin said he would meet Despallières's inner circle and be introduced to the company, although its main offices were in Los Angeles. His 'beau' would take him to FremantleMedia's four-day event to celebrate the end of the current *American Idol* series, one of the most successful television formats ever launched. It was at such events that Despallières picked up business for his social networking software venture, which he used to host video streaming sites for mobile phones.

Ikin confessed he didn't understand the work Despallières was doing from his apartment on iPhone applications: 'Something way above my pay grade, I'm afraid,' he told Gaff. The pressure on the obsessively organised older man was already beginning to show, for he added: 'You can imagine how I am with my life schedule already planned through to June 2009 but I have told him (and this could end up being a dealbreaker) I have existing commitments that I have to proceed with and if that means being apart for a while, well that's it, he also has to compromise.'

Ikin's communiqué went on to outline his travel plans, which were always made at least one year in advance. Due to his changed circumstances, he would now be unable to call on Gaff in the South of France the following month, but he still hoped to go ahead with his American tour during the four weeks up to 7 August and a subsequent visit to Crete with an Australian friend later that month. He concluded by saying, 'Hardest thing for me is sharing a bed after all these years of sleeping alone.' It was, he said, 11am at the time of writing and he was already exhausted since Despallières's work with people in the US meant he had to stay up most of the night to accommodate the time difference, with a diminishing packet of Marlboros always within arm's reach.

The missive from the other side of the world astonished Gaff. In reply, he wrote: 'Jesus. Too much for me to take in in one go. I do so hope it works out.' And mindful of Ikin's strict house rules – the Irishman added in capital letters: 'DO NOT NAG IF HE DROPS CRUMBS.'

The day after pouring his heart out to Gaff, Ikin rang a Sydney-based friend, Brian Flaherty, known to close friends as Faye, and invited him for elevenses at Yellow, their favourite coffee shop in the vicinity. When Flaherty arrived, he discovered that his friend had a companion: Alexandre Despallières. 'Peter explained that they had rekindled their friendship and that Alex was now a billionaire and had invited him to stay at his apartment on Central Park West in New York. I thought Alex was very charming and that he told great stories. He told me he owned not one but three apartments in the Central Park West block – one he lived in, another that he provided for his US personal assistant and a third that was empty at that time. He even invited me to spend Christmas there with him. It certainly sounded impressive. He showed me a photograph of a man he said was the grandson of Carlos Slim, who he also said was a close friend of his.

'A few days later we met up again for dinner at Peter's favourite restaurant and this time Alex had a companion with him – his name was Jérémy Bilien and, I must say, I thought the chap was a bit shifty.'

As the weeks went by, however, it was not dropped crumbs that were Ikin's chief cause for concern, but Despallières's declining state of health. There was further bad news: the Frenchman's doctors had told him he now also had two inoperable brain tumours. On 13 June 2008, Ikin wrote again to Gaff to advise him that their planned meeting in London would not happen: Despallières had been taken suddenly ill and was likely to need hospitalisation in Sydney. 'I may be panicking a bit – it's been very hard for me to see him suffering . . . luckily he has support staff here with him.' The 'staff' was the ever-present Bilien, or JJ as he was better known to the group now.

Gaff sent a sympathetic reply adding that he had been busy entertaining another friend, the Swedish actress Britt Ekland, a former Bond girl who had once been Rod Stewart's partner.

Facing death seemed not to be a big problem for Despallières. He had said he did not fear it and busied himself making arrangements for a smooth departure from this life. Both he and Ikin were familiar with family tragedy. Ikin's parents had died young, as had his sister Marie and all three of his brothers, twins

George and Bill, and Neville. Despallières's father, Marcel, had succumbed to a heart attack while the two of them were on holiday in the South of France in 2001. His mother, Monique, had died the following year, apparently by her own hand after failing to deal with the all-consuming grief of losing her husband.

There, however, the two men's similarities ended. While Despallières was something of a nomad, Ikin always regarded Australia as his home even to the extent of stipulating in a will he had made in 2002 that if he were to die abroad his ashes should be returned to Sydney and scattered in the harbour just as had happened with those of Ken East, the former managing director of EMI whom he regarded not only as a mentor but as a father figure.

It was for East that Ikin had first gone to work in the record business in 1970. 'Initially he was a sort of chauffeur and door-opener, but he built up contacts and became incredibly successful in the job,' says Roger Desmarchelier, who had been a close friend of Ikin's since they'd attended kindergarten together. Both were later enrolled at the Marist Brothers College in the prestigious Mosman district on Sydney Harbour's northern shores, just 5 miles north of the city's commercial heartland.

'His mother ran a tuck shop and she used to give me cream cakes because I was Peter's friend,' says Desmarchelier. Surprisingly, considering the success Ikin went on to achieve, he adds: 'As a boy, like me, he was lazy. We both left school before [our final exams] – in fact we were asked to.' But a lack of diligence that led to the premature end of his formal education soon vanished when the opening at EMI came his way.

Ken East's widow, Dolly, who used to run the press and publicity department at EMI Records, recalls those early days with great fondness: 'We always had a close friendship, and PI [as Ikin was affectionately known] did look upon Ken as a father figure.' It was Ken East who guided the young Peter Ikin through the early days of his career, and in the mid-seventies, when both men were working in London; it was East who suggested that Ikin return to Australia to manage the Motown record label there.

With East's sponsorship, in just a few short years Ikin had come a long way. Although extremely competent, and clearly passionate about the business, his success was due in no small part to his popularity. In a notoriously cut-throat industry, he had the rare ability to get on with everyone he met, and to put those in his company at ease.

As Dolly East recalls, 'Peter Ikin knew everybody who was anybody in the music business and they knew and liked him. He was unique.'

CHAPTER 3

THE MONEY-CHANGER

Having delivered his marriage proposal to the man he had just told he was dying, Despallières appeared to take a turn for the better, perhaps thanks to the Sydney sunshine. So, convinced that Despallières's complex health needs were, for the moment, no longer critical, Ikin was due to set off as planned for his summer trip to see friends in the Americas and in Europe. He would be leaving a seemingly recovering Despallières behind in the Elizabeth Bay apartment with Jérémy Bilien.

Before his departure, Ikin was reminded by Despallières that just around the corner was the 20th anniversary of their first meeting, and he said he wanted to give him a present to mark the occasion. His commemorative gift turned out to be something which seemed staggeringly valuable: a certificate for 500 shares – half the capital – in his IT conglomerate. There was just one piece of business that had to be transacted to make it 'all above board': Ikin had to give him in return a cheque for $50,000 to make it appear that he had paid at least some money for the billions of dollars' worth of stock he was being handed. In return

Despallières would give him a cheque for $50,000 and both cheques would be banked when the pair reunited in New York in August ('*and not before*', Despallières emphasised), so Ikin would, in effect, have paid nothing for the fortune he was receiving. A trifle complex, but it would all be legally watertight, his partner assured him.

The stock deal was to cause problems, however. Prior to his departure, Ikin checked his bank statement and discovered that Despallières had in fact cashed his $50,000 cheque. This was despite the firm arrangement that they would both hold off until they met up again several weeks later. He confronted Despallières about it and was alarmed to see the Frenchman fall at his feet in a convulsive fit. Bilien eventually revived him, declaring, 'Oh my God, Peter, that was a close thing.' Immediately afterwards, Peter dashed round to Brian Flaherty's apartment in floods of tears. 'He's going to die, he's going to die!' he shrieked in distress. 'Brian, why did I make such a fuss over a silly cheque? He's going to leave me his billions and I'm quibbling about $50,000.' After Ikin had calmed down, he told Flaherty the whole story, adding, 'We don't talk in Ms anymore, Brian, we talk in Bs.' He meant, of course, not millions but billions.

Despite an apparent reluctance to take on responsibility for Despallières's health care and the management of his fortune, Ikin was not averse to the prospect of inheriting riches beyond belief. Friends in Australia shared his newfound enthusiasm when he promised each of them a house. He also announced that one of his first purchases after he had inherited would be a private executive jet in which they could fly around the world together.

Soon after the incident over the cashed cheque, Ikin arrived in the Hamptons. He was spending his 62nd birthday with an old friend and former colleague, a financial expert who regularly advised the Australian on his business affairs.

During his stay, Ikin showed his friend the share certificate that made him the world's most unexpected paper billionaire. The friend, who does not wish to be named, says: 'I was also Peter's business advisor and, after we both retired, he would come out here and spend a couple of weeks with me to talk through his business affairs.

'Anyway, on this occasion he produced a document, showed it to me, and said, "What do you think of this?" It seemed to be a stock certificate for a substantial share in a company owned by Alex Despallières, but I have to say it didn't look like a proper stock certificate to me, more like something you'd pick up in an office supplies shop.'

Ikin explained the cheque fiasco, and that the whole exchange was for estate purposes. His $50,000 'purchase' of half of the company was a measure to prevent Alex's considerable fortune from passing to his brothers. As Ikin related the story to his old friend, he added that he had tried to cash the reciprocal cheque Alex had written to him. It had bounced. As someone who worked in the financial sector, alarm bells began to sound.

Ikin, however, was unperturbed, expressing the view that while Alex's affairs were extremely complex and were bound to present hiccups along the way, he was utterly trustworthy.

• • •

During his travels, Ikin learned of a new arrival at his apartment back in Sydney. Brian Flaherty, who called there regularly to check the mail, let him know that Despallières and Bilien had been joined by one Meg Sanders, an American woman whom Despallières had introduced to Flaherty as his New York-based PA. A bespectacled thirty-something with long, dark hair tied back into a ponytail, she seemed very much the sort of woman who was cut out for work rather than play.

'Alexandre told me Meg was such an important figure in his business world that he provided her with one of his New York apartments at Central Park West,' says Flaherty. 'Initially she was very cold but when I met her a second time, she was totally different and she apologised for her demeanour on the earlier occasion, explaining that she was jet-lagged after her flight from the US. But I think Alexandre had had a word and told her not to be so business-like. He is such a nice man.'

Considering Despallières's poor health and Meg's somewhat drab appearance, Flaherty was surprised to be informed by the men who took care of security for the apartment block that they were getting complaints from neighbours about the noise of 'wild parties' emanating from the Ikin residence and often spilling over into the grounds. The complaints centred on the comings and goings at all hours of the night and the sound of rock music being played from dusk till dawn. The concierge put it down to sour grapes on the part of older people who lived in the block and who were in bed by 10pm.

The disgruntled residents of Kincoppal did not have to put up with this for long, however. After Bilien spent a brief spell in St Vincent's Hospital in Sydney, having an operation for the removal of kidney stones, all three left Elizabeth Bay and, indeed, Australia, for the last time on Monday, 14 July 2008. Bilien was booked on a flight to Paris, where he was to have further treatment following his surgery at St Vincent's. It was in an email from Meg Sanders – a woman he had never met but who was to become his regular correspondent – that Peter Ikin learned that she and Despallières had embarked on a far more ominous journey. They were travelling by private jet – laid on by Carlos Slim – to Mexico, where the tycoon had arranged for Despallières to receive treatment for his growing brain tumours.

Ikin was shattered by the news. In an instant, his globe-trotting was stripped of all pleasure. He always kept his laptop with him so as not to miss the sporadic emails from Ms Sanders, giving increasingly gloomy news about Despallières's frightening condition and worsening prospects.

To give himself a little cheer he had googled 15 Central Park West, the Manhattan apartment building on the corner of West 61st Street and Central Park West, which was to be one of his new homes. The discovery he made was staggering: the starting price of apartments was $20 million ($30,000 a month to rent) with penthouses having sold to Hollywood A-listers and Russian and Chinese oligarchs for close to $100 million.

Just as he was wondering how much he would have to spend in tips (one resident had reportedly handed out $90,000 in gratuities in his first year), Ikin was greatly disappointed to learn from Sanders that Despallières's condition would not allow their planned rendezvous in New York to take place after all. He accepted, however, that his partner's deteriorating health had to take precedence over the joy he had anticipated in seeing this stunning apartment, and so Ikin carried on travelling until he reached London on 1 August. By now, he was gravely fearful of Despallières's chances of making any recovery and sent a plea to Mexico begging Meg for news. 'Every time the phone rings I hope and pray it's him just saying, "Hello my love, I am getting better, and I miss you."'

It begs the question: why didn't he fly to Mexico to be at Despallières's side? The answer seems to be that as much as he was troubled by the awful situation – and he was grateful to Meg for handling it all – part of him was dreading what lay ahead. Was his freedom worth the untold riches he had been promised? Was he capable of nursing, albeit briefly, a dying man? And besides, no one had requested his presence in Mexico.

On a less emotional note, Ikin realised from something Meg had written previously that she was keeping Bilien 'in the dark' about Despallières's grave condition. Ikin had been intending to travel to Paris on 7 August to visit Bilien and was anxious to know what he should impart to the assistant. Sanders responded the following day, beginning her missive with better news of the patient. 'Alex manages to focus to an extent that leaves me speechless. Yesterday he was talking with people from Google and a few minutes later was writing an editorial on Cuil – the new search engine that is supposed to beat Google. As usual, if it is work, everything seems to snap back into place, but as soon as it is personal, he will not talk and shuts down. But at least the injections are having an effect so that is good news and I wanted to share it with you.' She concluded by saying that she had withheld news of Despallières's condition from Bilien because she did not want to cause the latter added stress after his own operation.

Any comfort Ikin might have drawn from Sanders's relatively cheerful message was shattered two days later when he received another from her, striking a very different note. 'Alex makes progress and then slides back,' she began. 'Today he went for a walk – a crab-like walk because of the pain.' She had talked to the surgeons, but they had decided that an operation was out of the question; they feared he would not survive the anaesthetic, and even if he did, the surgery might do him more harm than good. 'His brain tumours are alarmingly big and unless the pressure diminishes his episodes will become more violent and more frequent.'

Despallières, she said, had granted her power of attorney and, since he was not in any fit state to make major decisions, she had decreed that surgery was not an option. In any case, he himself was fearful of any operation lest it render him a vegetable.

All they could do was monitor his condition and carry out his wish to be transported to the French Riviera whenever it became feasible.

The news must have crushed Ikin, and Sanders was keen to provide still more graphic evidence. 'He comes and goes, sometimes he is sharp as a tack and focuses on work then, all of a sudden he is in the far distant past and talking about things I have no knowledge of. Sometimes he speaks to me in French, crying and all I can do is to nod and hold his hand with no clue what is making him cry. But the doctors say that is the best thing to do, to let his mind work itself out, to go where it will and not contradict him . . . It's like a child playing with a light switch, on/off, on/off, 50 times a day interspersed with moments of great physical pain that morphine cannot ease. Last night he thought I was his mother.'

She went on to tell her correspondent that despite his unbalanced state, Despallières still remembered him – largely due to her daily reminders of his existence. If Ikin was in any doubt that his intended was going mad then that doubt was diminished when he learned that Despallières believed that the grand Mexican residence in which he was residing was his home and that his host, Carlos Slim, was one of his employees. Ironic, Sanders pointed out, because Slim would own Despallières's company once he exercised the options he had already purchased.

Ikin had made it known to Brian Flaherty that he had been growing increasingly irritated by Meg's lack of contact and her refusal to answer specific questions he had put to her concerning the state of Despallières's health. Flaherty confirmed that he too had been having trouble contacting Alex and Meg, so, in an affectionate email signed 'Faye', he asked Ikin to pass on his good wishes to the patient.

Suffering with insomnia, Ikin emailed Faye in the early hours after a day spent at the Dorchester Hotel's spa. Meg had, he conceded, answered some of his pressing concerns, even though he found them very upsetting; he was prepared for the bad news. He promised to contact his friend while travelling on the Eurostar on Thursday, 7 August.

Email became a lifeline for Ikin, who used it to send pictures of himself and Despallières to Meg, in the hope it would remind the failing patient of their relationship.

. . .

Although he was by now enjoying the familiar surroundings of his London apartment, Flat F, Cheyne Place, Chelsea, Ikin was sleeping badly. The two bedrooms in the basement of the split-level apartment were darkened by iron bars installed for security, but the gloominess did not bother him. It was the looming prospect of the civil partnership that was so troubling. It was, he considered, an irreversible step and he was plagued with anxiety. Was it the right thing to do? Did he really want what he was taking on? Could he run a vast empire? Could he care for a dying man? As one so fixed in his ways, could he cope with sharing his life with another?

Yet some of his friends thought it was Despallières who had the greater challenge ahead. Despite his warmth and generosity, Ikin was never going to be an easy partner.

Billy Gaff recalls: 'Peter was so particular and anal about just about everything. I cannot emphasise enough just how particular. You would go into his bathroom, and everything was laid out in straight lines. The toilet paper would be folded into a triangle at the end just like in a good hotel. Whenever I stayed with him in Sydney, he would make my bed to perfection, placing a teddy bear he'd bought specially – he knew I liked teddy bears – on the pillow. Once I caught him slipping into my room to plump up pillows I thought I'd arranged perfectly. So, on future visits I would make the bed with special care and then call out. "I'm ready for my inspection." He would call back, "I'm on my way, darling," and he'd walk into the room, take a close look and say perhaps, "Oh, that's very nice, you're such a good guest, but I like to fold the counterpane this way," and he would move it perhaps half an inch, and I'd say, "I'll try to remember that."

'One morning he came into the kitchen where I had just made myself some cereal for breakfast and he said, "Billy, what's this?" There were three cornflake crumbs in the sink, and I replied, "It's fucking cereal, Peter," and he made a point of cleaning the sink again. "Peter, what is it with you?" I said. "You've just spent a whole minute cleaning three little bits of cereal dust." I mean, the kitchen was [barely] used. I think I was the only one who ever cooked in it. He didn't cook – although on Sundays he would make bacon and eggs. But he would have splash guards around the frying pan and cook ever so gently to ensure that not a single speck of grease would land on the hob.'

Gaff's sister Miriam remembers another episode: 'Peter knew that Billy loved chocolate so one year when he went to stay, Peter put a large bar of the stuff in the fridge knowing that my brother would creep into the kitchen during the night to snack on it. On the second night when Billy went to find the chocolate bar again, it had been removed from its wrapping and broken up into squares which were arranged in a dish. When Billy asked why, Peter said, "Because, dear, the previous night when you broke yourself off some squares you left crumbs of chocolate on the floor in front of the fridge." That's how Peter was.'

According to John Reid, Ikin's life was very ordered, and he kept everything from receipts and letters to tickets and boarding passes from his travels. 'The last time I was at the Sydney flat Peter went into the kitchen to make some drinks and I picked up a magazine in the living room, looked through it, and then put it back down on the top of the pile. Peter came back into the room with the drinks and didn't say a word but picked up the magazine and put it back in the exact position I had got it from.' Notorious for planning ahead, his life would be mapped out. 'I'd say to him in June, "What are you doing for Christmas?" And he would give me his exact itinerary. He knew exactly where he was going, he'd booked the hotel rooms and the flights. He could tell you the airlines, the flight numbers, and the flight times. He'd always insist on reserving seat 2A on his flights and would likely refuse to fly if he didn't get it.'

'He was a terrible drama queen,' continues Gaff. 'For somebody who for most of the time was the nicest person in the world he could cause terrible upsets. If his wine glass was over-filled in a restaurant there would be a scene, he'd make the waiter take it away and bring back a fresh glass filled to the appropriate level. I remember once driving to Biarritz to collect him and bring him back to Cannes. We went for a meal at this very grand restaurant and he looked at the menu and snapped, "Nothing here I want." Then he called the maître d' over and said, "I want chicken," to which came the reply, "There's no chicken on the menu, sir." Peter by now was getting very cross: "This is a five-star hotel, there must be chicken somewhere, get me chicken." I tried to calm him down saying, "Peter, there are so many other things on the menu . . ." but he cut me off, saying, "Excuse me, dear, I'm speaking to the man in charge." Anyway, he got his way. They sent someone to another restaurant and got him his chicken.'

He may have been an intolerable partner but did Ikin like living on his own? Gaff didn't think so: 'I always found him to be a little bit lonely. He had lots of friends but, although he never said it, I always thought he was envious of others who had a partner.'

Yet given Ikin's character, some friends felt certain the romance was a passing fancy. John Reid was to say later: 'As far as the marriage thing is concerned, I thought that it would just blow over. I thought that Peter would come to his senses because he wasn't stupid. He was flattered by the attention of a young, good-looking, very charismatic man, and it's true that he was also carried away with this large amount of money he was going to get. I seemed to remember a figure of £8 billion being mentioned at one point.'

• • •

Even as the train whisked him to Paris for his rendezvous with Jérémy Bilien, Ikin's laptop signalled the arrival of an email from Sanders, in which she was clearly doing her best to further placate him by writing more about herself.

According to Meg, she was indebted to Despallières after he had helped her through a rough part of her life. Now it was her turn to return the favour as best she could. She suggested that in lucid moments Despallières was trying to do something professionally with Apple that could involve Ikin, and that there were moments when he could work, but mostly he was writing down his thoughts as his speech was failing. Sometimes he simply cried, Meg wrote.

Ikin arrived in Paris, where his meeting with Bilien proved to be awkward for both. At the modest apartment where he was staying close to the centre of the French capital, Bilien did his best not to discuss Despallières, and, mindful of Sanders's words of caution, Ikin also avoided the subject of the absent man's health. The meeting lasted less than two hours, but before he left, Ikin appears to have made a major decision. A single-page will was drawn up, dated 7 August 2008, to replace the one he had made in Australia in 2002. It was witnessed by Bilien and a young French journalist Despallières had befriended called Vincent Bray. It left everything to Despallières, although that was obviously moot as there seemed not the remotest chance of him surviving Ikin. It seemed a purely symbolic gesture.

On his return to London, Ikin made no mention of the new will to his friend Robbie Buchanan, who was staying with him, even though Buchanan had been a beneficiary of the 2002 will – and had been aware of this. Ikin was treating Buchanan, a fellow Australian, to a holiday in Europe and the pair met in London before setting off for Crete. While there, the pressure of the situation was beginning to show. Buchanan says: 'For the entire holiday [Peter] was terribly upset. He made constant phone calls to Meg Sanders to see how Alex was, and most of the time his calls went unanswered, and messages he left were not returned. When they were, Meg told him that Alex was delusional, and it would be best if he did not speak to him as it might upset him. Peter spent most of the holiday in his room crying. He was very upset.'

Following their return from Crete, Ikin and Buchanan joined John Reid for lunch at the elite Mayfair fish restaurant, Scott's. The matter of the chaos in Ikin's life caused by the arrival of Despallières and Bilien arose. 'Oh, my life's not my own since Alexandre came back into it,' admitted Ikin. 'The house is disrupted.' Reid later asked Buchanan what he made of it all and his reply was, 'Oh, Peter's happy, let him have his fling.' What Ikin had blurted out in that unguarded moment, however, was a further indication that he was far from happy about the direction his life was headed. And for too long he'd had no word of Despallières.

Despite his growing frustration at yet another lapse in communication, Ikin waited three more days before sending a deceptively casual email to Sanders that nonetheless anticipated bad news.

It took Sanders more than two weeks to send a reply, in which she confirmed Ikin's interpretation of no news meaning worsening news. Despallières's condition was 'pretty bad' and all she and the doctors could do was to make him 'as happy as possible as much as possible'. Throughout the ordeal, she said Alex remained the 'voice of hope'.

Heartbreaking stuff, but the big surprise was that Bilien had now joined them in Mexico, something he had assured Ikin at their meeting in Paris he had no intention of doing. A frantic Ikin had resolved to undertake the 12-hour flight to Mexico, booking a seat on a carrier that would speed him to Despallières's side. The travel plans, however, were short-lived. For now he was being told Despallières was about to travel to London.

While the seriously ill Despallières was being made ready for the arduous journey, Ikin was able to speak to him on the phone. It was not a happy experience. Despallières asked Ikin to call his mother (who had been dead for several years), and take her to join him in Mexico. When Ikin asked him how to contact her, Despallières gave him a telephone number for the Paris address at which Ikin knew he'd used to live. Surprisingly, the number still worked, but when he called no one answered.

During their brief conversation, Despallières had said that he wanted to stay with him in London but Ikin was concerned that his Chelsea flat was not grand enough for a man who said he had enjoyed the hospitality of two of the world's richest men – Carlos Slim and the Sultan of Brunei – and he wrote to Sanders: 'It's a much older/smaller flat (Victorian era) than my place in Sydney, still with 2 bed/bath but it's on 2 levels with internal stairs between the bedrooms downstairs and the living areas upstairs which may be difficult for him so have suggested that initially he go to one of the sultan's places until JJ [Bilien] can see if this place is totally suitable.'

* * *

Although Ikin had assured Despallières that he would enter a civil union with him, he still didn't seem entirely convinced about it himself. The more he considered it the more Ikin clung to his single status. He felt he was too set in his ways to change now. But he had promised Alex and besides, despite the complex drawbacks involved, there was the enormous financial advantage to be considered. He was, after all, only human. He had always been a high-flyer, but with the fortune from Despallières's bequest he would be able to live like a king and spoil his friends with riches beyond their imagination.

It was during one of his sleepless nights in London that he made his decision: he would go ahead and grant Despallières what the younger man had described as his dying wish. When morning arrived, he contacted the register office at Chelsea Old Town Hall to demand the earliest possible date for a civil union to take place. He was to learn, however, that it was not that simple: there were formalities to take care of, forms to be filled in, enquiries to be made. Ikin grew exasperated when told that the earliest possible date was 10 October. He grew angrier as he told the official on the other end of the phone how ill his partner was, that he might not survive until then. Alas, there was no reasoning with the registrar: 10 October – two days after Despallières's 40th (and undoubtedly final) birthday – it had to be.

• • •

On 2 September, Ikin joined Billy Gaff and his sister Miriam for lunch at Scott's. No mention was made of the wedding plans, but the group was in high spirits. In spite of Ikin's growing concerns over the updates he was receiving from Meg Sanders, it was clear to his close friends that he was looking forward to what life he and Alex had left together.

After lunch, the trio went back to the Connaught Hotel, where Gaff was staying, and ordered a bottle of their finest champagne. 'When my sister chastised me for ordering a whole bottle, Peter turned to her and said, "He can't take it with him, Miriam." I mention that because, sadly, those were practically the last words I heard my friend of so many years say because it was the last time I ever saw Peter face-to-face.'

When Ikin got back to Cheyne Place, he sent his friend an email to clarify his feelings, making it clear that he was over the moon about his relationship and utterly besotted by his French 'beau'. He wrote: 'Look, Billy, I know Alex doesn't have very long but if I can have three months of what you and Steve had I would consider myself a very lucky man.' It was at odds with what he had said to John Reid at Scott's only a few weeks earlier. Clearly Ikin was a very confused man.

• • •

Within days of Ikin's lunch with Gaff, Despallières arrived in London. His condition had improved immeasurably, and he astonished not only Ikin but others he met by his rudely healthy appearance. For a man who had just flown 5,500 miles and was within weeks of dying, he looked refreshed and amazingly well, although Gaff points out that there seemed to be peaks and troughs in his condition in the coming days: 'Yes, there were times when he looked absolutely fine but others when he was obviously extremely ill.'

Although it was nothing like as glamorous as Ikin's ritzy Elizabeth Bay apartment in Sydney, Despallières seemed perfectly content to stay at Flat F in Cheyne Place, and did not, as Ikin had suggested, move into one of the Sultan of Brunei's grand homes in the city. Situated on the ground floor of a red-brick Victorian townhouse on a residential street close to the Thames Embankment, the music mogul's London residence had the feeling of a home that was rarely used and never updated. The ground-floor drawing room and dining room had 1960s-style chain-store furnishings and were free of books and art of any quality. A dated dresser held the only ornaments: a small collection of plastic model aircraft. In the basement – reached by stairs once used by the coalman – there were two dark bedrooms: the one at the rear was the master bedroom since the one at the front was polluted by the noise of ever-flowing traffic on the nearby streets.

Nevertheless, despite the relative dimness of his surroundings, Despallières made no complaint and, instead of taking to his bed as expected, stepped up his social life, accepting invitations from those who knew and liked his host. On 13 September, the trio went to John Reid's birthday party at his splendid Mayfair home close to the American embassy in Grosvenor Square. When he wasn't charming other guests, Despallières was admiring the decor of the residence and couldn't help but contrast it with the dowdier surroundings at Cheyne Place. Despallières was in high spirits but both he and Ikin restrained themselves from mentioning their forthcoming nuptials to others. This was neither the time nor the place, and these were not the people with whom they wanted to share their secret.

CHAPTER 4

IN SICKNESS AND IN HEALTH?

Despite Despallières displaying robust health in public, behind the scenes Ikin voiced continuing concern for his well-being. On 17 September he sent an email to Billy Gaff: 'It's been a rollercoaster of a week, Alex (and Jérémy) have been staying with me for 2 weeks now. Last Friday his full memory returned suddenly – before he had been very confused, with him trying to call his long-dead parents etc. Then he had a few good days, we even went to [John Reid's] birthday party last Saturday at the house, drank a bit and had a great time.'

Ikin did not accompany him to any of his medical appointments but was satisfied by the details, however negative they were, which Despallières furnished him with after each one: 'Monday he had a bit of a meltdown so saw specialist today and after a CAT scan, it was not good news: tumours are aggressive in the brain again (the Mexican procedure was to provide short-term relief to enable him to travel and regain his faculties) and now he has problems with his bowels. He had hoped he/we would all be able to fly to New York on the weekend as that's where he wanted to be till the end but that is out of the question now, the *QM2* Sunday sailing (if space) being considered but concerns if he had episode or worse on the ship so doctors told him get his affairs in order fast and they doubt he will see his 40th on 8 October so he will stay here with me and Jérémy to look after him until the end (I don't know what to expect here and am very scared). That's what he wants, just for the 3 of us to be together.'

Clearly distressed, Ikin added: 'Just so sad for me, typing this with tears running down my face.'

Despite the gloom and doom, however, Ikin concluded his message to Gaff by adding a surprise: Despallières had not taken to his bed but was in fact 'at the Dorchester tonight with his friend the Sultan of Brunei!!! To see him you would not know there was anything wrong with him, which makes it all the sadder.' Both Ikin and Gaff accepted that this was merely one of the idiosyncrasies that went with Despallières's condition. Neither dived into the politics of the sultan, the owner of the prestigious Dorchester Hotel.

The following day Despallières was out to lunch again, even though his socialising was catching up with him and he did look somewhat the worse for wear. This time Ikin took him and Bilien to dine with John Reid at the celebrity haunt La Famiglia, a restaurant frequented by the rich and famous on the King's Road at World's End. Reid's own guest that day was the Jamaican-born singer/actor Peter Straker. And if Despallières seemed tired and had to be cajoled by Ikin to eat his meal, Bilien needed no such coaxing to have a good time. While Ikin was no doubt preoccupied by his lover's condition, Straker found reason to be deeply suspicious of the young Bilien.

As Reid relates, 'Peter [Straker], who was sat next to him, said to me afterwards, "That Jérémy boy kept flirting with me, rubbing my knee under the table."' Reid would have raised the matter with Ikin but thought better of it, and in any event, it was Bilien who was misbehaving while Despallières remained ever the gentleman, despite his condition on any given day.

Reid, himself an astute businessman, was nonetheless intrigued about Despallières's incredible success. When the Frenchman gave little away about his commercial activities, Reid's curiosity compounded. He made a note of the name of the website of Despallières's sprawling business empire and became determined to google it later.

· · ·

Having made the decision to go ahead with the union, Ikin was hesitant about announcing it. He had discussed his dilemma with no one, fearing deep embarrassment if whatever he had decided proved to be a mistake. He was still concerned about what others would think and remained reluctant to broadcast the news. The one person he knew he could confide in was Billy Gaff, so, on the morning of 1 October, he sent his best friend a guarded message: 'I want you to know that we are getting married in a civil union ceremony (his dying wish) at Chelsea Old Town Hall on the 10th, so just praying he holds on for that and his 40th birthday two days earlier. This news is just between us. Jérémy and Anne Marie Nicol [Ikin's former secretary] will be our two witnesses as required. So much paperwork to sort out . . . All going as best as can be expected. He is suffering with pain steadily increasing, so meds were upped which makes him very drowsy most of the time although at night he works on company biz and is still sorting out his estate matters with his French and US lawyers. I am a bit of a wreck but that's life and his comfort and happiness are my prime importance at this time. The last six months have been life-changing for me in so many different ways.'

He went on to assure Gaff that their long-planned cruise to the Galapagos Islands the following month was very much on. They would, as they'd planned so long ago, watch the whales and dolphins, see scurrying iguanas and basking sea lions. They would witness giant tortoises lumbering onto soft sandy beaches. Paradise was getting closer.

Gaff began his affectionate reply with an attempt to bring a smile to his friend's face: 'So at last we will be able to call you Mrs.' He went on to say how much he empathised with him, recalling the loss of his own partner, Steve Andrews, 13 years earlier, before ending on a practical note: 'Glad to hear Alex has a French lawyer as estates in France are tricky: the family cannot be excluded.'

It may have been something of a throwaway comment, but Gaff was on to something. French inheritance law has stiff provisions to ensure at least a portion of all estates are left to surviving family members, regardless of what appears in any will. Despallières must have encountered this law after his parents had died and would certainly have known it would be almost impossible to disinherit the problematic siblings entirely.

Convinced that the grim reaper was fast approaching as far as Despallières was concerned, in his next missive to his friend Ikin relayed more of what Despallières had told him about his 'evil' brothers and the responsibilities he was going to have to take over once Despallières had died: 'He is definitely on a downward spiral as expected but he tells me he will hold on to prove to me that his love for me can beat his pain,' he wrote late one night. 'Yes, the estate matters are tricky as he has two evil brothers who did terrible things to him when his parents died. One even forged Alex's signature on inheritance documents. His French lawyers have the full story and will fight like hell any [attempts] to contest his will above what may be required by French law.' When I contacted one of Alex's brothers he denied that there was any history of forgery in the estates of either of their parents.

Ikin's focus on practical matters strongly suggests that, although he was preoccupied with caring for his dying companion, romance was not much of an issue. While he made frequent references to Despallières's protestations of love for him, he rarely divulged any reciprocal feelings. He did, however, make frequent references to the material gain he stood to make once he became a widower. In his desperation to bring about the union, Despallières had afforded Ikin precious little time to consider his feelings, but he had certainly aroused his suitor's interest – and, indeed, whetted his appetite for the material changes the union would bring about. Ikin concluded his email to Gaff with these thoughts:

'If next Friday [the wedding day] takes place (and I pray it does) and his requests are followed I believe I become his heir and inherit – a frightening thought as I know what is involved – the company, copyrights (books, TV shows, movies etc.) property both residential (US and France) and commercial . . . I am going to need my own lawyers and accountants in the US and maybe here as well – just what I needed at my time of life!'

Always looking to poke fun at his friend, Gaff cheekily replied: 'Well, nothing wrong with being an heiress.'

• • •

The day before the big event, Ikin's curiosity on one matter got the better of him. He asked Despallières if he was finally going to meet his correspondent, the mysterious Meg Sanders. Had she been invited? After all, she had been writing to him for many weeks, not merely giving details of her boss's condition but offering personal information about her own role in his life. Peter asked the question in a matter-of-fact way but Despallières's reply was as brief as it was blunt: he did not want Meg there. She was in love with him and had always hoped that he would marry her. Her presence, therefore, would almost certainly cause 'a scene', so she had not been informed that the ceremony was taking place.

Ikin may have been shocked by the revelation that he had a rival for his suitor's affections, but he offered no comment. He had, after all, arranged a witness of his own and the ceremony, as far as he was concerned, was nothing more than a formality. It was beginning to look more like a case of taking care of business than a romantic commitment.

As if to emphasise his lack of emotion about the event, Ikin phoned Billy Gaff just prior to setting off for Chelsea Old Town Hall. 'Now listen, dear,' he began. 'I don't want any flowers, I don't want any fuss; this is all very low-key, and I don't want anyone other than you to know.'

Ikin called again after the ceremony to let Gaff know it had all gone well. 'They were drinking champagne in the flat and he was extremely happy. He laughed at a congratulatory email I had sent him. It read, "Jesus Christ, what are you going to do next?" Then I sent him a more serious one saying, "Look, should you be going on our trip to the Galapagos Islands leaving Alex in the condition he's in? It doesn't seem right."' Ikin replied in a typically detached, decisive manner, saying, 'We've discussed it, and Alex would be very upset if I didn't go. We've said our goodbyes.'

If Ikin was less than exhilarated by what had taken place, then his friends made up for it. When he emailed Brian Flaherty a photograph of himself with his arm loosely draped over the shoulder of his now-legal partner, with Bilien and Nicol in the background, the caption merely read. 'One of the photos taken at today's "happy event".' The addition of quotation marks around the last two words suggested a degree of cynicism. Flaherty responded in more glowing terms: 'Dearest Peter and Alexandre. How wonderful you look together. It makes me so happy to see two people I love so very happy.'

When, the day after the ceremony, he got round to replying, Ikin paid no heed to the sentiment conveyed in Flaherty's affectionate message. Instead, in a further move indicative of his businesslike approach to the whole affair, he took stock of just what the civil union had committed him to. He wasn't about to simply inherit a fortune, he had to *manage* it. He was to become president and CEO of Despallières's sprawling business empire and would have to take care of his many properties around the world, and the number seemed to be growing by the day. Then there were Bilien and Sanders to look after (Despallières wanted them both to have homes) and the 'evil brothers' to outwit. Although his retirement had been fulfilling, the challenge was taking Ikin back to the cut and thrust of his working days when he was king of the castle with a mile-a-minute lifestyle to match, and at first he undoubtedly embraced it all with vigour.

To set things up, Despallières explained that Ikin would have to go along with certain untrue statements to the authorities. Ikin would be required to state – wrongly – that he himself was domiciled in the UK and that Despallières had been a UK resident for the previous five years. If this proved successful, it would make his estate exempt from France's 60 per cent inheritance tax, meaning that Ikin would only have to pay the British rate of 40 per cent. In yet another statement demonstrating the couple's preoccupation with the financial side of their arrange-ment, Ikin wrote in an email to Flaherty: 'He says he is moving his personal assets here (better hurry) and will set up joint bank accounts for us and that the billions from the sale of his company is his personally and will not go through the company's books.'

Ikin said Despallières had destroyed his existing will and 'wants me to cancel my Australian will which doesn't mention him and do a new one here (I'm not sure about that)'. This was a strange sentence indeed, in view of the document he was alleged to have signed in Jérémy Bilien and Vincent Bray's presence in Paris, just two months earlier.

The dying Frenchman also wanted his new legal partner to put his Chelsea home in their joint names, but 'this will take a long time so it will never happen', wrote Ikin. He also confided that it was all getting a bit too much for him, especially since he would be required to run the part of Despallières's US business that would not be sold off to Carlos Slim, 'and that has major difficulties for me being an Aussie'.

The real-estate side of Despallières's estate was even bigger than Ikin had initially believed, with five residences in New York, three in Los Angeles and two in Paris. Then there were commer-cial properties in many American states, Canada and Japan.

'I don't know how I am going to cope but I don't want to let him down. He also wants me to give JJ [Bilien] ownership (with me) of one each of his New York and LA apartments, that will become solely his on my death, and also to move Meg Sand-ers from CPW [Central Park West] to another of his apartments and give her two years rent free. After all she has done for him, I would be inclined to give it to her.

'So, you can see there is a lot of uncharted territory for me. I really don't know how I am going to do it and keep an eye on the company as well and now he tells me he thinks his CFO (finance) guy is shifty, but he could run rings around me on finance stuff, so that's a worry. Each day as he fades a bit more it just gets worse for me for the future.'

Although there is no record of it, Despallières must have spoken to Sanders on the night of the civil union for, according to Ikin's email to Flaherty, he had told her that not only was Ikin going to be her new boss but he was to inherit everything. However, he had still not informed her of the civil partnership they had entered. 'She [Sanders] may have hoped that he would marry her,' Ikin added. 'I need her to stay at her post in New York and run the ship.' Other than Gaff, Buchanan and Flaherty, Ikin still did not want anyone to know about the civil union. Despallières agreed, adding that if it became public knowledge his brothers could say it was a ploy to stop them from getting their share of his fortune, which, under French law, they would be entitled to if he died a single man.

Back to business, Ikin went on to tell Flaherty that, in an effort to convince his staff that he was well and everything was 'running normally', Despallières had asked his marketing department to set up meetings and presentations for him in New York the following month, knowing full well he would not be able to attend them.

On a practical note, Ikin declared: 'He knows about the Galapagos trip [with Gaff] next month and still wants me to go saying [by then] he will have gone away on his permanent vacation . . .' Clearly both men had accepted the hand that fate had dealt them.

An exhausted Ikin concluded the missive: 'The more it unravels the worse I get, just took the first Valium of the day – even before breakfast – to keep me calm.'

• • •

True to his word, Billy Gaff kept his friend's secret even after the wedding had taken place. The only person in whom he eventually confided was his sister. Miriam recalled: 'Billy rang me up in a state of great excitement. "Peter's a Sadie, Peter's a Sadie," he kept saying. It took a minute or two for the penny to drop then I worked out what he was trying to say. "Sadie, Sadie, Married Lady" is the song Barbra Streisand sings as Fanny Brice in the movie *Funny Girl*. "Sadie" was the slang term used for a married woman in the New York Jewish community in the period in which the film was set.

'"You mean Peter's got married?" I asked. "Yes, yes," said Billy, who was obviously very happy for his friend. "Peter's a wife now."'

On his wedding day, Ikin told Despallières he had gone ahead with provisional arrangements to accede to his request of putting his Cheyne Place flat into their joint names. 'It was my wedding present from Peter,' Despallières subsequently claimed.

Four days later, Ikin converted his Barclays premier international banking account into a joint account but deposited only a small amount of money. The bank duly issued a new book of cheques on which the signatories were named as 'Mr P.A. Ikin & Mr A. Despallières'.

A fortnight into the partnership Ikin discovered he had not simply acquired a partner – a situation he had never experienced before – but had sacrificed far more than he'd bargained for. He was no longer master in his own home and, as a man who was used to having everything placed just as he wanted it, that clearly annoyed him. It seemed to be getting worse by the day as Despallières began to treat his partner as a manservant, expecting Ikin to do all the housework at Cheyne Place.

Ikin's annoyance came close to boiling over on the day he found himself obliged to leave the apartment because Despallières said he was going to have a meeting with David E. Kelley, creator of the *Boston Legal* television series for which he said he wrote scripts, and it was imperative he had the place to himself. When Ikin returned to his home sometime later, Despallières was alone but wearing a new gold watch that he said was a gift from the grateful producer. Yet again, Ikin bit his tongue, but added it to the list of matters that would need addressing once the newness of their status had worn off. For his part, Despallières chose to ignore Ikin's simmering anger. This was the way things were going to be from now on.

On 24 October 2008, Ikin filled in an application for a Schengen visa, which would have allowed him as an Australian national to travel freely around Europe. On the form he stated that the principal reason for wanting the visa was to enable him to make short-stay visits by train to Paris 'to be with my partner of civil partnership, Alexandre Despallières'. Somewhat surprisingly, Ikin gave Despallières's address in Paris as 1 Quai Voltaire – the home address of Despallières's close friend, the eminent French lawyer Olivier Metzner. It raised questions for Ikin: if his partner lived there with the older man, then had they been what the gossip writers would call 'an item'. Was this a ménage à trois?

Ikin put the thought out of his head. He would not question his new partner on this issue. After all, whatever had gone on in Alexandre's life before they'd committed themselves to each other was none of his business.

Besides, he had to take care of other matters. By the end of the month Ikin had become even more concerned about his corporate responsibilities and the tax liabilities of being in control of such a huge fortune as Despallières's. On 30 October he had a meeting at Ernst & Young, one of the world's top accounting firms, to resolve the most worrying issues of his looming tax situation. In an email to his mentor Ken's widow, Dolly East, he outlined the solutions explained to him: 'I am to become a UK resident again in this tax year and pay tax after next April on monies I have brought in from Jersey as I have no direct income (salary etc.) here in the UK but don't have to pay UK tax on other income/interest earned in Jersey, Switzerland or the US as long as I don't remit it here. So am relieved to have all this sorted as long as Alex and our civil union hopefully exempts him from paying inheritance tax (40%) here in the UK on his estate or at least monies he has here at the time. Sounds very complicated but will leave it to the lawyers and accountants to sort out. Love, PI.'

Despite his expression of relief, this was not what he wanted at this stage in his life. All the extra worry and Despallières's increasingly poor domestic behaviour was getting to him, not to mention the lies this honest man was having to tell to tie everything together. The day after sending that email, he went ahead with his Schengen visa application. The document he signed on 31 October was witnessed and sealed by a notary solemnly declaring that 'Alexandre Renaud Marcel Despallières . . . has been living here with me at our principal residence since his arrival in the United Kingdom in September 2007 and will continue to do so for the future following our Civil Union Partnership which took place on 10 October 2008 at the Register Office of Chelsea Old Town Hall, King's Road, London SW3.'

As a man who throughout his life had done everything by the book, this would certainly not have sat easily with Peter Ikin. He had always been scrupulously honest in his own dealings with record companies and artists. Even in restaurants, he was known to consult a pocket calculator to work out exactly how much tip he should leave based on a precise percentage of the bill. Falsifying the Schengen application to fit in with Despallières's financial planning was adding to his uncertainty about the wisdom of having gone ahead with the union, and complex financial planning compounded doubts now swirling around his mind. It was not, however, something he confided in his partner: Alex was too adroit to allow matters of conscience to get in the way of business planning. And after all, Ikin reasoned, he wouldn't have made billions in one short lifetime without an element of dishonesty. What billionaire ever had?

CHAPTER 5

THE RELUCTANT GROOM

Despallières's departure with Bilien for Paris, where he said he needed to attend to legal matters with Metzner, allowed Ikin a few days of solace. It gave him time to think things through as well as affording him an opportunity to hook up with some of his old friends. On 1 November, a quiet Saturday, he went to the cinema. When he got back to an empty flat, he noticed that John Reid had called him. He responded with a text message: 'See U called but no message, have been to the movies (Alex is in Paris) call U later, P.' Then he picked up the phone and called Brian Flaherty in Sydney. 'He was on the phone for half an hour,' says Flaherty. 'He said he was thrilled to have the apartment to himself because Alex was in France seeing his lawyer. He also said he couldn't wait to get on the boat to the Galapagos Islands with Billy. For the first time in a long time, he seemed in excellent humour.' The dying Despallières's absence gave him a brief interlude in which to relax.

Meticulous as ever, Ikin outlined his plans for the next six days in another email to Dolly East in Sydney: 'I am going to

Brussels tomorrow to see friends [Roger and Gay Desmarchelier] and then on Thursday on to Paris to spend time with Alex and am due back in London next Monday (10th). If required will be contactable on my mobile during this time.'

The following morning he sent an email to the Desmarcheliers to say that he was on the train and would call them once he arrived. True to his word, he telephoned Roger from his room at the Royal Windsor Hotel at 2pm and arranged to meet the couple in the hotel's downstairs bar three hours later. When they arrived, the Desmarcheliers found Ikin already installed with a bottle of his favourite Laurent-Perrier rosé champagne chilling in an ice bucket at his side.

He seemed unusually hurried with his normally effusive greetings: he had, he said, something to show them, and with that held out his left hand to display the Cartier ring they and others were quite familiar with. 'We'd seen it before,' says Roger, 'but never on that finger.'

It was his way of telling them he was no longer single. 'He went on to say that he and Alex had married in a civil ceremony a couple of days after Alex's birthday.' Roger was struck by Ikin's manner as he made his revelation: 'I have to say that at no time did he seem excited or even enthusiastic about the news he was delivering. He was very relaxed about what he was saying and was at pains to point out that he had wanted to tell us face-to-face rather than in an email.'

The Desmarcheliers were taken aback at their friend's relatively formal announcement of his change of status: 'He could see that we were surprised at the suddenness of his decision since Alex had only come back into his life a few months earlier. Having known Peter for a very long time we were happy for him although we got the feeling that he was not as happy as one would expect him to be in such a situation.'

After producing his camera to show his friends the few photographs taken of the ceremony and the modest celebration that had followed, Ikin clearly decided he had dealt with the matter and ordered a second bottle of Laurent-Perrier. Then he talked about Despallières's health issues and, as if he had an agenda of items to be discussed, moved on to the burden of inheriting his partner's billions – a topic which inspired the Desmarcheliers to offer any assistance he might require with the huge financial responsibility he was facing.

The trio stayed in the bar for quite a while and as the conversation progressed Ikin confided that he was far from happy about the way his life was changing: 'He said he wanted "all this" to go away. He wanted to get back to his more relaxed, planned way of life.'

The champagne had relaxed Ikin by the time he ordered a taxi to take them to the restaurant he had chosen for their dinner. There the conversation turned to the host's forthcoming cruise to the Galapagos Islands and Ikin's eyes lit up at the prospect of three weeks in the company of his trusted friend, Billy Gaff. It had, he said, taken two years to plan the trip down to the last detail. 'He was on his way to Paris the next day to meet Alex but needed to get back to London a few days later to get his clothes packed and ready for his departure for South America on the 13th.' For Ikin, it all had to work like clockwork.

Now somewhat maudlin, Ikin relayed the events of the previous spring, giving the Desmarcheliers a detailed account of how Despallières had turned up on his doorstep, talked of his imminent death and his yearning for them to be wed. Roger and Gay knew the story well. They remembered the lunch he had joined them for at their home in Sydney back in May: 'Alex had rung several times that afternoon. Peter appeared quite agitated. I don't think he was sure he wanted to commit himself to what Alex wanted, especially his wish that Peter and he live in America.'

As the Brussels meal progressed, lubricated with two bottles of wine, Ikin became less discreet. He told his friends that in the run-up to the civil union ceremony he had been obliged to pretend that they had been in a long-term live-in relationship in the UK, and that he had not only been paying all the live-in expenses of the so-called billionaire sharing his life but had also put his Jersey bank accounts into their joint names in order to create a financial picture of long-term togetherness.

Then Ikin – his courage perhaps fortified by the wine – dropped something of a bombshell. He announced that once in Paris he was going to demand of Despallières that he sign a bank form removing him as a signatory to the accounts. 'He stressed this several times,' Desmarchelier declared.

The husband and wife noticed that their friend was not looking in the best of health. He had lost weight and told them he was not sleeping properly, 'as Alex was sick a lot of the time and there was real pressure in the day-to-day household due to his terminal illness'. Now speaking more liberally than he had in the hotel bar, he told them that he found it necessary to slip out of the apartment secretly from time to time, 'to escape the tension'. He found that lunching with friends, going to a cinema or even window-shopping allowed him to forget for a few precious hours the nightmare that his once-well-ordered life had become.

As Ikin paused to ponder the inevitable death scene that lay ahead, Gay Desmarchelier asked him if he had prepared for Despallières to have palliative care in his final days, but she was told almost abruptly, 'Alex doesn't want anything like that. He doesn't want strangers looking after him and particularly doesn't want other members of the gay community to look after him.' Even as he uttered the words, he came to realise that his partner and Bilien were being selfish in that respect and he said that, once he reached Paris, he was going to confront both men over the palliative care issue and, he added, as a relatively incongruous afterthought, their untidy living standards in his home.

Just as suddenly as it had moved to such sombre matters, the conversation switched to finance, with Ikin detailing once again what he was about to inherit. Then yet again reared the ugly head of French law, which would deflect a great deal to the two brothers whom he said Despallières despised.

'Peter did not seem happy about being drawn into such a complicated financial situation. He was unhappy about the impact it was all going to have on his own life when Alex died, given the volume and diversity of his assets,' says Desmarchelier. 'He wanted to get things back to normal and make his own decisions about life and in particular his travel plans. Incidentally, Gay is a nurse and always asked him about his health, level of fitness and eating habits when we caught up with him. This time was no different and he assured her that he was looking after himself, although he was a bit strained by the Alex health trauma.'

Ikin's immediate travel plans were limited to his journey to Paris the following day – the city where, he told the Desmarcheliers, Alex would be awaiting him after spending two days with his French lawyer signing papers. He was looking forward to having his first sight of one of Despallières's impressive portfolio of properties, for he was to stay in one of his partner's luxurious apartments.

Their farewells just before midnight were markedly affectionate. 'As we parted company, Peter put his arms around Gay and me in a big hug and said, "Jeez, I love you guys." It was unusual to see him so emotional.'

It was as if he had unloaded a burden.

According to staff at the Royal Windsor Hotel, Ikin was in fine spirits by the following morning. Showing no ill effects from the wine and champagne he had indulged in the previous night, he duly set off for Brussels's Midi/Zuid station late on the morning of Thursday, 6 November. There, decked out in his stylish cashmere overcoat and sporting a gold neck chain and the diamond stud he always wore in his ear, he boarded the 12.37

train for its 82-minute journey to the French capital. On arrival, he made his way to the Hotel Abba Montparnasse located on the Rue de la Gaîté, next door to the risqué Bobino nightclub in the 'cultural' heart of Paris. It was far from the five-star Hotel George V situated in the city's Golden Triangle where he would normally have luxuriated. Word had reached him that Alex had booked himself into the Hotel Abba while an apartment he owned was being refurbished. Despallières was to say that his downsizing was a favour to his lawyer and close friend Olivier Metzner who, he said, part-owned the hotel.

Putting his disappointment about the accommodation downgrading to one side, Ikin's determination to resolve pressing financial issues with his beau became ever more urgent, particularly the matter of removing Despallières as co-signature from his banking arrangements.

But as he neared the hotel, Ikin had no idea that Despallières was aware of his intention, having been able to read the older man's emails.

As he cast a disparaging glance around the hotel's modest lobby, Peter Ikin was utterly unaware of the tragic scenario that would soon unfold at the Abba.

CHAPTER 6

DEATH IN PARIS

Answering a call from the hotel's management, the first responder was a fireman, Cedric Bruxelles, who sped to the Abba Montparnasse on the morning of Wednesday, 12 November. There, in room 37, he found the bulky body of Peter Ikin lying naked on his bed, one lifeless leg hanging over its side. Bruxelles's notes record that there were two other men in the room – Jérémy Bilien and a man who he thought was the young journalist Vincent Bray but was more likely to be Despallières. An initial examination of the corpse indicated that the man he had been summoned to attend to was in cardiovascular and respiratory arrest. An emergency call to SAMU (the service d'aide médicale d'urgence) precipitated the arrival of a young doctor who formally pronounced Ikin deceased, and he began to write a death certificate. After fireman Bruxelles drew the doctor's attention to a bag full of medicine in the room and some other small medicine bottles and tablet casings lying empty on the bedside table, the doctor added a note to the certificate, recording suspicion of suicide or homicide as possible causes.

The emergency services' summons to attend to Ikin at the Abba Montparnasse was by no means the first they had received during his brief stay. Indeed, a little more than eight hours after his arrival at the hotel on Thursday, 6 November, to be reunited with his partner of just 27 days, Ikin was already requiring medical attention following a fall on the stairs outside his room. When the Brigade arrived on that occasion, they discovered the 62-year-old sat in the hotel hallway; he had escaped with only a slightly bruised lower left leg. Their subsequent report said he seemed cheerful but not drunk. Ikin, who could not speak a word of French, was attended by a woman who fitted the description of Meg Sanders and a man who described himself as the victim's nephew and who translated for the casualty. They were subsequently joined by Despallières.

Satisfied that their services were no longer required, the emergency men went on their way. However, in the early hours of the following morning they were recalled to the hotel. This time Ikin was in his room, throwing up. His 'nephew' said he had summoned them again because his 'uncle' was bringing up blood. Fireman David Salle said that although their patient appeared 'snoozy' he had, apparently, drunk only one glass of wine. According to Salle's notes, Ikin refused to go to hospital, and his 'nephew' passed off the incident by explaining that Ikin was a cocaine user. When shown photographs later, Salle said he thought the man who had said he was the victim's nephew was Jérémy Bilien. Salle had been mistaken in his initial identification of Vincent Bray as the other man, who was not in Paris at the time.

Later that morning the Desmarcheliers sent Ikin a text message to thank him for the 'lovely night' the three of them had spent together in Brussels just 36 hours earlier. Uncharacteristically, Ikin had not replied. Nor did he respond when the message was repeated two days later. He couldn't. Ensconced in his depressing hotel room, he was growing sicker by the hour.

At around 4am on Saturday, 8 November, the emergency services were summoned yet again. Fireman Freddie Marlier discovered Ikin in his room in a state of some distress, sobbing intermittently. Also in the room were a woman, and a man who said he would translate for his 'uncle'. Between sobs and through the self-appointed interpreter, Ikin said he was suffering terrible headaches and that he had vomited. Fearing that he might have suffered head injuries in the fall two nights earlier, Marlier insisted he go to hospital for tests.

Ikin resisted at first but finally agreed and, along with Despallières, Bilien and a woman, was transported to the emergency department at the Hôpital Cochin, renowned for its public assistance work as well as being the city's major burns unit. Although the fireman said he had not observed any drugs in the room, Marlier reported that the 'nephew' – who he also said matched a picture of Jérémy Bilien – again insisted on making the point that the victim was a drug user.

Despallières was later to tell Billy Gaff that at the hospital Ikin had become abusive, had assaulted a porter, and had had to be sedated. When he regained consciousness, he was in a restraining jacket and he shouted at doctors to free him. Once the straitjacket had been removed, he tore away cardiac leads attached to his chest and demanded to be released. After warning him that, unless he remained for treatment, he might die, the doctors – according to what Despallières told Gaff – demanded that he sign a form freeing them of all responsibility. Barely able to write his name, Ikin obliged.

Back at the Abba, Despallières telephoned Ikin's former secretary, Anne Marie Nicol, in London and told her he did not know what to do. All the time Ikin was swearing at him for making the call, finally grabbing the receiver to swear at Nicol before hanging up.

Despallières was later to claim that at this point Ikin contacted his doctor in London and arranged an appointment to see him the following day, as well as making a Eurostar booking to get him there, but the doctor insists that call was never made and says he hadn't heard from Ikin for more than three years.

Staff and guests had never seen anything quite like it at the Abba, a boutique hotel which boasted 59 'quiet and comfortable' contemporary rooms. Situated in the heart of the Rue de la Gaîté and conveniently close to the Gare Montparnasse, it has since changed its name to Hôtel Le M. But for that weekend's residents, the drama was not over yet.

On the evening of Tuesday, 11 November – a bank holiday in France – police records show that a Red Cross volunteer, Clement McCarthy, was called to the hotel where Ikin had fainted. Again, there were two people with him who this time were subsequently identified by the observant McCarthy as

Despallières and a woman who gave her name as Sandrine Gaillot.

The man from the Red Cross reported that the reasons for Ikin's condition were unclear but his companions stated that he appeared to have consumed large quantities of paracetamol, either to ease the pain from his fall five days earlier or perhaps to alleviate withdrawal from drug and alcohol consumption. Ikin refused to go back to the Hôpital Cochin where Despallières said he had been a victim of theft (his diamond ear stud was missing), but instead was driven to the emergency room at the Pitié-Salpêtrière, a teaching hospital which once specialised in the mentally disturbed and criminally insane poor of Paris. Despallières was on hand to translate into French whatever the Australian said to the doctors. The doctors, made aware by Bilien (who presented himself as Peter's boyfriend) that Ikin had taken a large amount of paracetamol, then carried out blood tests which confirmed high levels of the drug in his body.

Bilien signed a discharge document on Ikin's behalf, and then Peter, the unwilling non-French-speaking patient, was once again allowed to return to the hotel – a journey that was to be his last. After they rowed yet again, Despallières booked a separate room for himself at the hotel and said he retired to it only to be told some hours later that his partner had been pronounced dead by the doctor summoned by fireman Bruxelles. Despallières was inconsolable and collapsed weeping, while repeating to anyone who would listen that he would have donated his liver to keep Peter alive.

After a long wait demanded by the police as they investigated the doctor's direction that the death should be treated as suspicious, Peter Ikin's body, covered and bound to a stretcher, was finally carried unceremoniously from the lobby of the hotel to a waiting van provided by the IML (L'institut médico-légal) before being transported to the morgue. There a cursory autopsy was carried out. Despite the doctor's notification of 'suspicious death' affixed to the paperwork he had written in room 37, the resulting coroner's verdict decreed that death had been caused by heart failure and hepatitis. The body was then duly released to Ikin's partner, Despallières, for burial. At this point Ikin's closest friends knew nothing of his passing or how this tragic episode had unfolded. As word slowly spread, they were shattered to hear the shocking news.

The dead man's loved ones in Australia were also informed and, despite their grieving, they reminded Despallières that Ikin had expressed in his will a wish that his remains should be returned to Sydney, the city he loved so much. Apparently oblivious to their wishes, Despallières barely waited until Ikin's autopsy had been completed, the day after his death, before organising a hurried cremation to be held just a week later. A handful of the dead man's friends scrambled to reach Paris in time, as the widower had only notified them the night before. One witness described the farewell service as a 'pauper-like' ceremony in a damp, cavern-like room beneath the Cimetière du Père Lachaise, France's most famous cemetery, which was founded by Napoleon and where the remains of Jim Morrison,

Oscar Wilde and Édith Piaf were interred, albeit in much grander circumstances.

'Weather-wise it was a miserable day anyway,' recalls John Reid, who had rushed there from London with two of Ikin's other friends, Paul Northcott and the Australian actor Simon Burke, to pay their respects. In doing so they almost doubled the number of mourners. 'We sat in this cold miserable room with Peter's very large coffin positioned in the centre. There was no music, no priest, and the room was very dark. A man came in from a side door, said something in French, which I certainly didn't understand, and then left us to it. Alex, dressed in a very smart suit, sat weeping alongside Jérémy Bilien and the rest of us remained there for a few minutes in some discomfort. This did not seem the right way for such a beloved man to go, a man who had achieved so much and who had so many loving friends around the world.'

This was a far cry from the grand farewell that Ikin had envisaged in his beloved Sydney, saying goodbye to his friends to the haunting sound of Elton John's song 'Funeral for a Friend'.

After an uncomfortable few minutes the mourners got up one by one, each placing a flower on the coffin before making their exits. They had lunch together at a nearby bistro, then Reid, Northcott and Burke, having said their goodbyes, caught the train back to England, still in mourning.

Apart from his internationally spread family of friends, there was only one surviving blood relative to mourn Ikin's passing, Father Gary Perritt, a Catholic priest who was the son of Ikin's late sister, Marie. The priest – who these days sports a Cartier watch once given to him by the dead man – incurred Despallières's wrath when on 8 December he conducted a funeral service (sans corpse) at St Canice's Catholic Church in Elizabeth Bay before hosting a reception at the Cruising Yacht Club across the water – both venues that had been used for the send-off of Ikin's good friend Ken East. Surely a more fitting memorial for such a great man.

Despallières was not invited, although he insisted later that he would have chartered a plane to get there and carried Ikin's ashes with him.

· · ·

Despallières rushed back to London to the dead man's Chelsea apartment and on the night of his partner's cremation decided that there was only one way to get over a funeral – to have a party. A party, as it turned out, for three. He went on the internet to find a companion to help himself and one other pass the night there. Via a site that specialised in catering for those with such needs, he made contact with an escort, a young man called Lucas who lived not far away. When he arrived at Cheyne Place, the willing participant, who was born in Germany but raised in Wales, was surprised to discover it was to be a threesome, but as he said later, 'Hey-ho, the more the merrier.' Nor was he shocked when he was told the nature of the sex that was required – something he claims even he had never experienced before.

Not happy with just the financial reward he was given for his night's work, the escort, clearly besotted with Despallières, subsequently made numerous attempts to be reunited with his new client, only to discover that he had been given the number of a mobile phone Despallières no longer picked up calls from. He left numerous messages over the next few days, all of the same nature: 'Alex, why don't you pick up the phone? Why won't you return my calls? I gave you my heart, how could you treat me like this?'

For the time being, however, this tryst was to remain Despallières's secret. Despallières then set about playing the sad widower with the dead man's close-knit group of friends in London.

CHAPTER 7
TAKING ADVANTAGE

Once comfortably settled into Cheyne Place, Despallières turned his attention to his benefactor's friends – most notably Gaff and Reid – inviting them around to share his grief. Exercising the charm for which he was well known, he had no difficulty in mustering their presence. Although they knew precious little about him, they felt sorry for him. He had been Peter's beloved friend. It never struck any of them as suspicious that he had been present when Ikin, a healthy man for his age, had died so unexpectedly.

On Billy Gaff's first visit, Despallières insisted on showing him a briefcase that had belonged to Ikin, and was at pains to demonstrate that he knew the combination. It had, he pointed out, been ripped open from the back and the contents – a little money in various currencies and some papers, he said – had been removed. There were no visible signs of forced entry to the flat so he considered it an 'inside job', carried out by someone who had a key. However, he said he had taken the precaution of reporting it to the police, who 'didn't seem interested' as there had been no apparent break-in.

On reflection, both Gaff and Reid (to whom he also showed the briefcase) agree that Despallières's behaviour seemed odd. For a man in mourning he seemed to be making a big fuss about something as trivial as a broken briefcase. Gaff and Reid had no idea why, but they were not about to challenge a man who had just lost his partner and whose own life would soon come to an end.

Despallières also made a point of showing Reid the will Ikin had made in Australia in 2002, in which he had left his estate to be divided between Father Perritt and a few friends and charities in Australia. He appeared to know nothing about the will his partner had made in Paris just four months earlier, in which he was the sole benefactor, even though Bilien, and his friend Vincent Bray, had witnessed it.

Concerned for the newly widowed Despallières's well-being, Reid threw a lavish 'cheer-up' dinner party for him at his Mayfair home three weeks after Ikin's death. To his host's relief, Despallières appeared to be enjoying a recovery. 'He looked fantastic that night. He turned up in a floor-length black leather coat lined with mink which must have cost at least £10,000, and he ate like a horse,' says Reid, who had his cook prepare risotto with truffles followed by fillet steak coated in foie-gras, all to be washed down with fine vintage wine. To keep the conversation going Reid had invited a small circle of friends, including his former chef Graham Carpenter, the socialite Howard Malin, Brian Clivaz, a well-known figure in elite hotels and hospitality, Billy Gaff and, of course, Jérémy Bilien. Reid made a diary note afterwards of the location of the grand apartment Despallières talked of in New York – 15 Central Park West – because he was keen to rent one there himself for a forthcoming stay in the city.

Although they still mourned their recently departed friend, the group lavished attention on his surviving partner and, overall, it was a happy occasion. Reid believed that Despallières's good mood indicated that his health had turned a corner and he was ready to get on with his life.

Because Despallières said he enjoyed 'the company of the ladies', Gaff would often take his sister Miriam and occasionally his friend Britt Ekland along with him on his daily visits to Cheyne Place. Miriam recalled: 'Billy called me one day and said Alex was pleading with him to bring me to the flat. So I went and he greeted me with hugs and kisses. "Oh, I'm so happy to see you," he kept saying. He was the same with Britt, although it has to be said that she was bowled over from the very first time she met him for dinner. She said she could hardly eat for looking at Alex because he was so beautiful.'

Gaff, who became a daily visitor to the flat, said, 'I drove him to wherever he wanted to go and that included the London offices of a firm of solicitors. I believe he had literally picked them out of the Yellow Pages [telephone directory]. It was my understanding that he was only trying to find out what his rights were under the civil partnership.'

On one occasion, when Gaff met Despallières's solicitor, the group were having dinner at the Cheyne Place flat: 'We had been talking about probate and Despallières said that Peter was domiciled in England, and I said I didn't understand that. He said it was "documented". I'd certainly never seen it but it was odd that I was the first one to raise that Peter was not domiciled in England.' Under Gaff's questioning, Despallières explained that he had discovered a document, signed by Ikin, declaring that he lived in the UK. 'It should have raised a flag as a person's residence and domicile are not the same,' says Gaff, with the benefit of hindsight.

By this point Ikin's new will, made in Paris on 7 August 2008, had also surfaced, though again Gaff couldn't quite fit all of the pieces together. It seemed odd to him that the two witness signatories – Jérémy and this Vincent Bray – were sleeping with Alex. Gaff also questioned the 'robbery' at the flat. Although Alex told everybody he'd reported the theft to the police, an inspector from the local station later swore in an affidavit that no such report was made. Fortunately for Despallières, a photocopy of the document turned up in Paris, presumed to have been taken when Ikin had signed the original.

Such revelations did raise questions in the minds of Gaff and Reid, but for the moment everyone was more concerned for Despallières's health than any legal dealings, since it appeared to be in a continuing downward spiral. He was growing thinner by the day and complained about being sick throughout the night. One night he became so desperately ill Gaff rushed him to the Chelsea and Westminster Hospital, but he refused to be admitted. Gaff subsequently engaged the services of a private doctor who prescribed medication, largely to sedate him.

• • •

Impressed by the splendour of John Reid's Mayfair home, Despallières decided to do something about refurbishing the Chelsea apartment he was in the process of inheriting. Ikin's lack of interest in the place was evident wherever one looked. 'It really was pretty awful; [furnished in] bad taste,' said Billy Gaff's sister Miriam, 'rather like a run-down three-star hotel. I believe Peter bought it furnished and never acquired anything decent for it. Why should he have? He bought it as an investment and only used it for sleeping on his occasional visits to London.' Ever keen to help, Miriam and Billy agreed to take Alex on a shopping trip to buy some decent furniture.

Before he could start spending, however, Despallières wanted to open a new bank account, and lost no time in doing so. Choosing a bank close to his new home, Despallières – accompanied by Bilien – walked the short distance from Cheyne Place to a nearby branch of HSBC. There he was met by a woman – one Mirella Iacurci – who had encountered him briefly two months earlier when he had called to enquire about banking there but had broken down sobbing before any business could be done. On that occasion Bilien had explained to startled bank staff that his friend 'has just lost his partner, it's the funeral tomorrow and he is very upset'.

On his next visit, in January 2009, however, he was in far better spirits as he sought out Mrs Iacurci and asked her if she remembered him. He went on to explain that he was now over the death of his partner, declaring, 'Life has to go on,' and asked about opening a premium account. When Mrs Iacurci explained that he had to lodge £50,000 to have such an account, Despallières said he thought he could manage that by transferring to HSBC money he kept in an account with Barclays, so an appointment was set up for him to meet the branch manager.

On the day of the appointment, Despallières arrived punctually and was shown directly into the manager's office. After several minutes, during which Despallières bizarrely produced papers to show that he had once been adopted (and more of that later), the manager emerged into the banking hall and demanded of Mrs Iacurci, 'Do you know who that man is? He's a millionaire, a multi-millionaire!' He returned to his room to confirm to his new, very wealthy client that the bank would be delighted to have him as a premier account customer, but Despallières was not to be easily placated: 'They're googling me out there, aren't they?' he asked. 'Your staff are checking up on me. Well, I don't mind, I've nothing to hide. Just tell me I will get a new cheque book for my premier account without delay.'

But it seems Despallières didn't have the necessary money at hand. Bilien later took Gaff to one side and asked him if he would lend Despallières £50,000 to enable him to open a UK premier account, for the transfer of the substantial funds he could bring in from America. Gaff's response was to offer a simple solution: 'But he doesn't need a premier account because he can transfer funds using my American account.'

When that conversation was relayed by Bilien to Despallières, it precipitated a highly charged reaction. 'That evening I got a call from a sobbing Alex,' says Gaff. 'He said that I had let him down, that in effect I had accused him of being a liar, and that as a result he was going to quit London and go back to Paris. He made me feel so guilty that I agreed to lend him the £50,000 and made a bank transfer to his HSBC account for that amount the following day.'

When the cheque book arrived at Cheyne Place, Despallières went into another rage. It had on it the address of HSBC's branch in the Surrey town of Haslemere, where he had lived before mixing with record industry high-flyers, a humble address with which he no longer wished to be associated. In his anger he demanded the account be closed, saying he would take his business elsewhere. Only the gentle Mrs Iacurci was able to calm him by apologising profusely on the bank's behalf and assuring him that the wrong would be put right.

Before Despallières could set about improving his new home, he had plenty to keep him busy. For a start, there seemed to be a never-ending flow of visitors. One of the first to arrive after 2009 had dawned was a woman from Paris who he introduced as 'my very good friend Sandrine Gaillot', explaining to friends that 'she helps with various aspects of my business operations in France'.

The odd thing about Gaillot – considering she assisted an international businessman of Despallières's standing – was that she spoke only in French. 'It was all a bit uncomfortable,' says Gaff. 'I would say something to her, either in English or my pidgin French and Alex would translate it for her and then translate her reply into English for me. At least that's the way it was for the first couple of visits. Then the third time I went round during her stay, she suddenly spoke English with a strong American accent. I was astonished.'

Gaff confronted her about it, asking, 'But aren't you French?' 'No,' she replied. 'I'm American.' 'Then why did you go through that whole charade of pretending you couldn't speak English?' Alex replied for her: 'We were playing a joke on you, Billy.' But Billy was not amused. It left him feeling uncomfortable, with some of the trust he had placed in Despallières eroded. Smarting from a perceived humiliation, he withdrew his support for a while.

Playing games on people became something of a familiar pattern in Despallières's behaviour. He seemed to enjoy deceiving others and then pretending it was all a joke. 'That was funny,' was a phrase he used endlessly, apparently oblivious about the offence it might cause when the joke was made at someone else's expense. Having established this as a trademark, he was free to utilise it whenever he was caught out in something he said that later proved to be untrue.

Gaff managed to overcome his annoyance at what was the first (but would not be the last) example he witnessed of

Despallières's odd behaviour. He resumed his daily visits to Cheyne Place, sometimes accompanied by Ekland, who frequently sympathised with the handsome single billionaire over the recent loss of his partner.

Feeling sorry for his friend's widower, Gaff cooked, cleaned and shopped for him, although he was later to complain good humouredly, 'My mothering side was exploited!' Whenever he spotted something the flat needed he bought it, and that included a washing machine, a dryer, and a daily supply of fresh flowers – Despallières liked to have a spray of white roses, replaced every two days, beside the urn containing Ikin's ashes, which he kept on his bedside table.

Gaff was spending so much time at Flat F that he would often remain overnight, sleeping on the sofa until Despallières offered him the spare bedroom and he duly moved into it with the clothes he always kept in London. Now in his mid-sixties, it hardly matched the comfort Gaff was accustomed to, and it was only later that he could find an explanation for the move. Months afterwards, Gaff conceded: 'I was obsessed with him, sympathised with him, and was angry with him – occasionally all at the same time.'

Although Gaff was used to more salubrious living quarters, the arrangement seemed to work; if a problem arose, Despallières usually suggested a solution. For example, when Gaff complained about the problem of parking his new Mercedes in the nearby streets, where parking for non-residents was extremely hard to come by, Despallières had the answer: as a resident, he would apply for a parking permit. All Gaff had to do was to transfer the vehicle's registration documents into his name. It sounded simple and it worked. Gaff was pleased. It was, it seemed, a problem solved.

Gaff's cooking skills were legendary in his circle and almost every night he prepared gourmet meals for Despallières and whichever members of his entourage happened to be around. 'Despite his illness and his slight build he managed to put away a fair amount of food, but he would never eat dessert,' says Gaff. 'Whenever the main course was finished he would go downstairs to the bathroom to brush his teeth and that would be it. I must admit I was a bit puzzled about that because I made fabulous desserts.'

The ever-obliging Mr Gaff was not the only one the Frenchmen could turn to in times of trouble. On one occasion when Gaff was out of the country, John Reid took a telephone call from a desperate Bilien saying, 'John, Alex is really ill. I've got to get him to a doctor.' Reid says, 'I was aware that Alex had HIV and I know people at the John Hunter Clinic next door to the Chelsea and Westminster Hospital, so I got him fast-tracked there. He went and they were fascinated by his case because he had survived the illness for 20-odd years apparently without taking any of the medication available. Anyway, they expected to see him again but he never went back and they had no way of making him do so.'

Concerns were growing in Reid's head: he knew of too many people whose lives the illness had claimed. Why had

Despallières failed to take his medicine? And why would he not return to the care of the doctors who wanted to help him? Alas, Despallières made it clear he had no wish to discuss the matter. Says Reid: 'On my few visits there was a lot of sobbing and when I asked him questions Jérémy would do the answering and he would always say, "Alex is so tired he can't talk." That wasn't much help because I saw Jérémy as what I would call a street boy. I've no idea if he ever had a job; as far as I knew he was Alex's assistant – at least that's what Peter told me. I never took much notice [of Bilien].'

• • •

Although his poor health was obviously of great concern and he was already living on borrowed time, Despallières had another, more immediate problem. Despite his apparent wealth, he had no ready cash. He explained to Gaff that his fortune was tied up with the £10 million Peter Ikin had left, and that the beneficiaries of the will Ikin had made in 2002 had managed to freeze everything by challenging his claim that their civil union made him Ikin's sole heir. Gaff did his best to persuade his younger friend that civil unions were not recognised under Australian law, but Despallières insisted that Ikin had become domiciled in the UK and the estate was therefore governed by English law, which permitted him to inherit and would untangle his own fortune in the process.

Meanwhile, Sandrine Gaillot had returned to Paris to visit her mother, a grand old lady who, she said, lived in a splendid apartment opposite the Israeli embassy. Her return on 22 January was marked by yet another dramatic episode in the life and times at Cheyne Place.

Gaff had been in Wales with Britt Ekland: 'We returned to Chelsea at around six in the evening and Sandrine came in very soon after us. We hadn't been there all that long when she got a phone call. Well, you've never heard hysterics like it! She was shouting and screaming. Her mother who she had left only a few hours earlier, had been found dead at their home in Paris. "Mama! My mama!" – she kept screaming it over and over again.'

After a while, Sandrine began to calm down and went around the flat lighting candles. 'We broke out the champagne and she drank a lot of it "to celebrate my mother's life", she said. Then, they – Alex, Jérémy and her – all sat around talking about the newly deceased mother.' Mme Gaillot had apparently been a stunning woman who had spent much of her life on the stage. She was also extremely wealthy and, as Despallières told Gaff, had left behind many properties and Swiss bank accounts that Sandrine was going to have to look after and sort out. The group continued to reminisce into the early hours of the following morning, and at 6am, Gaff took Sandrine to the station so she could catch the Eurostar back to Paris, to arrange her mother's funeral.

Amid the turmoil, Despallières decided the one thing that would help to relieve the scent of death was a cat, and what Alexandre needed Alexandre got. Gaff agreed to buy him one, and money would be no object. At the time it was possible to purchase a cat for something in the region of £30. It was at a cost of £320 that the all-black Ratatouille was purchased from a cattery close to Heathrow Airport. Nothing but the best was good enough for a billionaire pet owner, so Bilien was dispatched to Harrods to purchase a cart for the Cheyne Place newcomer so he could be wheeled around. Although he had played no part in obtaining the animal, Despallières appeared to be besotted as soon as she arrived, and afterwards would go nowhere without her.

Despallières's next move was to send Bilien to Paris to obtain a photocopy of Ikin's new will, of which he (Bilien) and Vincent Bray had been the witnesses. It would only be a photocopy, Despallières explained, because the original had been stolen from Ikin's briefcase at the flat while he'd been in Paris arranging the funeral.

Since it was only a one-page photocopy seemingly made in Paris by Ikin on his day trip to see the ailing Bilien, the beneficiary might have anticipated some problems in getting probate without a thorough investigation being first carried out. However, there seemed to be no undue difficulty, and probate, conditional on the original will being produced, was granted. The official proving of the will meant Despallières was eligible for almost immediate receipt of £3.8 million (of an estimated £7 million) in cash and to take ownership of Flat F in Cheyne Place, which, despite its shabby decor, was worth at least £2 million.

He had to wait just six weeks before Barclays was able to release the cash, and even after this point Billy Gaff (who had no idea that his friend had secured Ikin's money at this stage) continued to fund his spending. After all, there was no reason to suspect that Despallières was anything less than a fabulously wealthy man who would quickly repay his debts. Gaff's sister Miriam recalled: 'I went round there one day and Alex was studying the brochure for a lovely house in Chelsea. The price was £8 million and he said it would cost another £10 million to get it like he wanted it to be. I said, "Alex, it's huge – why do you want to buy a house so big?" And his reply was, "Because I can afford it."' Miriam did not raise an eyebrow: true or false, the remark was very much in Despallières's style and dismissed any challenge to his grandiose plan. The bigger the sums, it seemed, the less likely anyone was to doubt them.

* * *

February saw the arrival of another Frenchman at Cheyne Place: Vincent Bray, co-witness to the newly discovered Ikin will of 2008. Despallières introduced the new arrival to Gaff as a journalist who had a very big job in television and was in London to meet his bosses the following day at Joe's Café in South Kensington. Alas, it seemed Bray's luck was out, for when Gaff drove him and Despallières to the well-known eatery the following day, the 23-year-old went in alone and quickly returned to say his bosses had not turned up. Later Despallières whispered in Gaff's ear: 'He is actually Jérémy's estranged boyfriend and I am trying to bring about their reconciliation.' Gaff shrugged his shoulders – it was none of his business, but was he getting too close? He was growing tired of being used as a lackey.

With so much going on, the residents of Cheyne Place decided a break was called for, and Billy Gaff had just the place – a magnificently converted stone barn set deep in the Rhondda countryside of South Wales. So, on a bitterly cold March morning, Alexandre Despallières, Jérémy Bilien and his boyfriend Paul Smith, and Ratatouille the cat, along with Peter Ikin's ashes, joined Gaff aboard a first-class carriage on the express train to Cardiff where the legendary pop-star manager and the IT billionaire (plus his entourage) would travel to the valleys to spend a week dining on local lamb and trekking around popular tourist spots.

For a short while, all the grieving Despallières's needs seemed to have been taken care of, but then came a demand from his solicitors for £8,000 of legal fees. Gaff paid up.

Soon after, another demand was made for money. This time for £27,000 for Jersey taxes in connection with probate on Ikin's will, and despite Gaff's questions about how they could possibly have got probate in an English court on an Australian man's will, he once again brought out his cheque book.

As Easter approached, Despallières was growing restless and decided on another trip to Gaff's house in Wales. So, on Good Friday (10 April 2009), the accommodating host – still believing that his new friend's days were numbered – once again transported him to the Valleys. This time the party included Vincent Bray (but not Bilien or Smith) and, of course, the two things Despallières would not travel without: the cat and Ikin's ashes. Despallières made good use of the trip, reinforcing in Gaff's mind the intensity of his relationship with Peter Ikin, spelling out more details of his huge empire, and expressing sorrow that he would not be alive long enough to enjoy his good fortune.

No sooner had this incongruous assembly returned to London than Gaff announced that he had business requiring his attention in Jersey. 'Can I come with you?' asked Despallières. 'I need to talk to the people at Barclays there who are holding Peter's money.' Gaff's eyebrows were raised when Despallières said he was talking about some £47 million: 'I was astonished. Peter and I often talked about our resources, and he would say, "I'm not as wealthy as you, Billy." Yet the sum Alex had mentioned far exceeded my own financial worth. Peter tried to live on the interest on his capital, which he told me amounted to about £120,000 a year after tax, but Alex said this was wrong, that Peter had been successfully investing in property over the years and owned two other Chelsea apartments in Tite Street.' Gaff was surprised but still had no reason to doubt Despallières's assertion.

Refreshed by their Welsh sojourn, the duo set off to meet the money men of the Channel Islands. Once there, Gaff set off for his bank, Allied Irish (AIB), where he'd been a customer for more than 20 years. Prior to their trip, Despallières had said that since Gaff had spoken so highly of AIB he wanted to move his own money to it. Not such a good idea, he was told, due to the poor shape the Irish banking system was in at that point, but he was insistent, so he went along that day too, dressed in a very expensive hand-tailored navy-blue suit. During the meeting in the manager's office, he sprung a surprise by expressing a wish that they should have a joint account – a wish that shocked Gaff, who would never have entertained such an idea, regardless of the proposer's riches. He went on to describe his vast wealth and when the assistant manager, Darragh Hare, asked him how much he wished to bank with them he said a ballpark figure would be 'about $200 million'. A vast sum, which prompted Gaff to think it might be another of his 'jokes'.

No forms were filled in for the proposed joint account, but they were each given one to study and complete at their leisure. Then they went to Barclays where Despallières insisted on conducting his meeting alone. The following morning the Frenchman – in fine form – said he had filled out his AIB joint account form. Gaff had not done the same; he had no wish to surrender his financial independence as his friend Peter Ikin had done. Yet he knew that saying so would result in an exhausting emotional outpouring from Despallières. So as to avoid such a confrontation, Gaff purposely spoiled his own form. On the way to AIB for their second meeting, Despallières's mood suddenly changed to sullen. It was, he explained, because of the heavy-dosage morphine tablets he was taking. The mood did not bode well for a conducive meeting at the bank, especially when he lapsed into child-speak after being told he would need to provide proof of probate, which he was carrying, and a reference from his solicitor. Despite being urged to present the document by his solicitor, who was on the phone from Brighton, Despallières refused, and the meeting ended in chaos with Gaff losing his temper and shouting at the Frenchman for wasting everyone's time.

Gaff reflected on his impression of Despallières's solicitor. They had first met when Gaff had dropped Despallières off for a meeting with him in London. On Gaff's return to his car, he was surprised to find him sitting inside with Despallières. 'So I'm meeting the great man who managed the great Rod Stewart,' was his opening remark as he shook Gaff's hand through the open car window. 'I have a band of my own which you should hear. We're only amateurs but we're very good.' And when he next turned up for dinner at Cheyne Place the solicitor brought tapes made by his group and dominated the dinner conversation with talk of his plans to be a rock star rather than a solicitor.

Back at the Jersey hotel there was an unpleasant scene as Despallières began sobbing uncontrollably, saying that no one understood what he was going through. 'I felt awful,' says Gaff. 'After all, he was so ill, and now it seemed I had made matters worse. I sent him an email from my BlackBerry apologising for shouting at him and I promised it would never happen again.'

Ultimately, their friendship was fatally damaged by another row shortly afterwards. As soon as they returned to London it emerged that the Chelsea property had been insured by both men. The duplication would have been a nuisance, if not illegal.

'You can't insure it twice,' declared Gaff.

'But I've seen nothing to show me you had already done it,' Despallières replied.

'So you won't take my word for it that the flat is insured?' Gaff asked. 'You know perfectly well I wouldn't lie to you.'

'Oh, Billy,' Despallières responded, 'why do you get so upset?'

Gaff believes that Despallières had a reason for engineering the row, but at that stage he couldn't be sure what it was. He took himself off for a beer and when he returned Bilien had been summoned and was there to act as back-up for his boss. Despallières began to abuse the man who had taken care of him for several months so Gaff went to the room he'd been staying in, packed his things, and left for the final time.

They were to meet just once more: 'I telephoned Alexandre to recover clothes and some jewellery left at the flat, including a pair of valuable cufflinks with a 3-carat emerald surrounded by diamonds in each. "Oh yes, I will find them," he said. "They are in the safe." And then he said, "Oh, wait a minute, the safe has been moved to one of the other apartments Peter left to me in Tite Street. But I will get them for you." I was going to Cannes and said I would like to see him before I left. He agreed but he did not want me to go to Cheyne Place because he said the place was in a mess: some television sets had arrived – a gift, he told me, from a friend, who had an important job at FreemantleMedia, the company that marketed *The X Factor* and *America's Got Talent* among others. I had met the man previously at Cheyne Place and listened to him ask Alex questions like, "How is your house in Los Angeles?" "Do you still have your big contract with Apple?" Questions which appeared to back up everything

Alex had boasted about. I think he must have been in love with Alex at one stage. I didn't know anybody who wasn't in love with Alex; he was that good at sweeping people off their feet.

'Anyway, instead of going to the flat I was to join him at Starbucks in the King's Road. When I got there, he said it had not been possible to get my jewellery because there was some problem with access to the Tite Street apartment. He had a photograph taken of him embracing me in the street which he emailed to me on my birthday a few days later.'

With Gaff out of the picture, Despallières decided he needed someone to advise him on how to handle his fortune and called round to the local HSBC branch where he approached Mirella Iacurci, offering her a job as his 'investment manager'. She recalls: 'He said he wanted me to manage his financial affairs. He knew my mother was ill and said: "Come and work for me. You won't have to work full time and I will pay you more than the bank does." He was very persuasive, and anyway it was a good offer, so I accepted and went to work for him, initially at Cheyne Place.'

CHAPTER 8

SUSPICIONS AROUSED

And that's where I came in.

On 4 May 2009, I received a call from a highly distressed Billy Gaff – a close friend of me and my wife, Gerri. Sounding like a broken man, he said he was at his house in Wales, and between sobs asked if he could come and stay with us. He sounded drunk and was clearly in no fit condition to travel, so I told him to stay where he was. I packed an overnight bag, bundled our two dogs, Jack and Charlie, and their beds into the car, and drove 130 miles to Talbot Green, the town where he had his current UK home. Stuffed with high-end paintings and furniture, The Barns, with its exposed walls, vaulted ceilings and full-length arched windows, was where Despallières had so recently enjoyed Gaff's hospitality.

As I sped west along the M4 heading to Wales, I found myself thinking long and hard about my friendship with Billy. Of all the journalists writing about people in the music business, I'd been a latecomer to his circle, as I was to John Reid's. The two of them would meet up on their artists' world tours, but my friends in the music world were of a different school – the Beatles, Tom Jones, the Bee Gees et al. At that time, I had never met either Rod Stewart or Elton John. Our paths simply never crossed. I met Billy when I was invited to the mansion he then owned, close to the Berkshire village of Finchampstead. For the benefit of a Sunday-newspaper magazine, he was hosting a lunch to which he had invited several music luminaries. And me. As the show-business columnist on a national newspaper at the time, I was always a useful guest to have around when people had crumbs of gossip they wanted to drop.

We were good friends from the start. As we shared a dry sense of humour, our exchanges were often caustic. 'Don't worry,' said his then-publicist Tony Toon, 'it'll get worse.' He was right, it did. We frequently dined out together in the West End, taking it in turns to go to his favourite restaurants (which were always excellent) and mine (which he invariably said were rubbish). Wherever we went, the drink would flow and ideas would come bursting out from both sides. One such occasion was when Edwina Currie, then a government minister, incurred the wrath of farmers and egg producers after expressing a view that eggs produced in Britain were likely to carry salmonella. Billy clapped his hands in the air and declared (so loudly that fellow diners could hear what he had to say), 'I've got it. We've got to get her to do a cookery book, with eggs in every recipe.' In high spirits, I telephoned Mrs Currie at the House of Commons and told her it was imperative we meet that evening. 'But I can't,' she said. 'I've got to attend a committee meeting.' I wouldn't take no for an answer and she agreed to meet at 7pm 'providing it's somewhere close to the House of Commons but somewhere I'm unlikely to bump into any of my fellow Members'.

I nominated the bar at Dolphin Square, overlooking the fact that a number of MPs actually lived in the complex. When we all entered together and she saw the very people she needed to avoid, she turned first scarlet and then on her heels, and left. That was the end of Billy's egg cookbook idea. I was never sure which Billy enjoyed most – hatching the plot that had a senior politician at our beck and call, or knowing how it had almost ended in disaster for Mrs Currie. He has always had an impish sense of fun about him and I remember that when it became known that Edwina was the mistress of Prime Minister John Major, he called me and jokingly (I hope) suggested, 'Now we can kill two birds one stone – do the cookery book with the pair of them in the kitchen wearing aprons and showing the world how to poach!'

He was also the author of a famous telegram (supposedly from his client Rod Stewart) sent to Elton John who had just announced his plans to marry Renate Blauel at a time when he was enjoying a hit with the song 'I'm Still Standing'. Many people were surprised by the heterosexual pairing. Billy's wire read: 'You may still be standing, dear. But the rest of us are on the fucking floor.'

Gerri and I enjoyed many happy outings with Billy. We holidayed with him at his splendid apartments in Bangkok and Cannes, and had keys to the Welsh house where we were encouraged to stay whenever it suited us. It was never all sweetness and light, however. My arguments with him often ended in blazing rows when neither of us would give in to the other's point of view, and sometimes ended in tears (his) when the emotional music mogul failed to get his way.

Billy, however, had one good friend with whom he had never seriously fallen out: Peter Ikin. One of my few meetings with PI took place at a dinner party Billy gave at the house he was then living at in Wandsworth, south London. I noticed that Peter was smart enough never to rise to the bait when the conversation became contentious. When our host slipped away to the kitchen, Peter whispered to me, 'I think the world of that man. I know he can be difficult but I love him to bits and I will never allow myself to fall out with him. His friendship is far too precious. Remember that.'

Such memories were still racing through my head as I made my way up the Rhondda Valley towards the small town Billy had decided to make his UK home, largely because his lawyer niece, whom he held in high regard, lived nearby. A left turn onto a bridge that crosses the River Ely took me up a country road and to the huge iron gates that separate The Barns from the rest of civilisation, just as the owner liked it.

Though modestly named, the nineteenth-century house is a palace without rival in the area. Its metre-thick stone walls give the impression more of a fortress than a home.

* * *

The Billy Gaff who answered the door when I rang the bell was a man I hardly recognised. He had clearly been drowning his sorrows and was in a state of great distress, although at that stage I had no idea of the cause. He was clutching a bottle of Dom Pérignon in one hand and one of vodka in the other.

'Which one for you?' he asked.

'Neither,' I replied. 'I'll make us both some coffee and then we'll talk'. He put down the bottles and hugged me as the tears flowed from his reddened eyes.

And what a conversation we were about to have. Sat on stools around the oversized kitchen island while we sipped our drinks (mine was coffee, his the champagne he had proffered at the door), I listened to a tale of unimaginable woe. An investigative journalist of more years' standing than I cared to admit to, I was shocked to hear of the substantial amounts of money he said he had parted with and now feared he might never recover. But even now, emotion was clouding his rationale. In his mind Alex was still the good guy, the desperately ill man who had built a huge fortune, who needed care, attention and understanding. Billy was torn between his fondness for the vulnerable man and his suspicion that, somehow, he had been deceived.

Recounting the bizarre tale seemed to sober him up and, as the shadows grew longer on the manicured lawn outside, he began to prepare dinner. Billy's meals could be relied upon to match those of any Michelin-starred chef. The preparation was always meticulous and a joy to watch, although he would never tolerate any help in the kitchen, which he would call interference. He would spend hours preparing sauces and painstakingly recorded what he had in the freezer by way of trimmings. Once I asked him why he held on to the elasticated shower caps provided by the luxury hotels he stayed in. 'When you put food you've cooked away in the fridge, what do you cover the containers with?' he demanded crossly. Ever the perfectionist.

Sleep did not come easily that night. Assigned to the Blue Room – one of The Barns' ludicrously comfortable and spacious guest rooms – I lay in bed trying to work out just what I had walked into. Frankly, it looked a mess. Billy Gaff was a highly intelligent man with a radar mind. He knew pretty much everything there was to know about fine wine, art and literature – he could quote huge chunks of Dylan Thomas from memory. He also possessed a detailed knowledge of the law. Yet he had allowed himself to get into such a ridiculous situation. Had his emotions got the better of him? Had he substituted himself for his close friend Peter Ikin? And what of Despallières? Was he truly fond of Billy or had he simply used him, another wealthy man, to fund an extravagant lifestyle? Did he even despise him for slotting so well into Ikin's role in his life? Angry though he was at how the ungrateful Despallières had dispensed with his company, Billy was not ready to answer such questions.

They were, however, questions I felt obliged to find answers to as I walked Jack and Charlie across a Welsh hillside the following morning. Intuitively I felt this was going to be a long ride; just how long and how rocky I could never have imagined.

After a few days during which Billy and I talked through the fine details of his association with Despallières, the dogs and I returned to London, leaving him to sort his affairs in Wales. I was surprised when soon afterwards he followed us back to the capital, and more surprised still to find he had not learned his lesson. His emails to Despallières now went unanswered, but Gaff had a new correspondent: Jérémy Bilien, who was now living in north London with his boyfriend, Paul Smith, whom he'd met online at the close of 2008. In an unexpected development, Vincent Bray had moved into Cheyne Place with Despallières, and out of respect to his new companion, Despallières had moved Ikin's ashes from the bedside table to the back of a cupboard. The urn was now positioned next to a pile of sexual paraphernalia including a stack of pornographic magazines, brought into the house by Despallières, who either didn't realise that the ashes were inappropriately placed, or didn't care.

Bilien suggested he and Gaff should meet and 'talk things through', whereupon Gaff took him to dinner at Le Méridien Piccadilly in the West End. The excitement of eating at the next table to one occupied by the singer Beyoncé clearly went to Bilien's head and he drank far more than was good for him, though that was not an uncommon happening in his life. Just prior to passing out, he asked if he and Paul Smith might be allowed to spend a short break at the Gaff apartment in Cannes. Generous to a fault – and Cannes-bound himself – Gaff not only agreed but also paid the airfares for Bilien to travel to the Riviera with him, and for Smith to follow a few days later. The two men certainly could not regard themselves as his friends – indeed Gaff did not care for either man – but they afforded him an ongoing connection to Despallières, which he clung to. It was once said of my friend Billy that anything he let go of had claw marks all down it.

During his Cannes stay, Bilien told Gaff that Despallières was going through another bad health patch and had no available money to pay his doctor's bill (Gaff had engaged the services of private specialist Dr Eoin Waters). Gaff placed a call to Despallières and told him not to worry: in addition to settling Dr Waters's £1,400 bill he was advancing him a further £10,000 for HIV drugs, which, he was convinced, Despallières would repay the moment his Jersey money came through. Despallières thanked him and said he needed a further £5,000 for probate of the will in Australia, where he was inheriting Ikin's Elizabeth Bay property. Gaff rang the solicitor to say that the required £5,000 was on its way to him. He then had one more item of expenditure to shell out for: a bicycle for Bilien's use while he was in Cannes. It transpired the PA to a billionaire was penniless. Gaff believed that this was the way Despallières kept control, that while he provided for all of his staff's needs, he kept them on a very tight leash.

There was, however, dark drama ahead. Paul Smith had turned up in Cannes and while Bilien was sleeping off a wine-filled evening in the guest bedroom, Gaff fell into a midnight conversation with the new arrival as they sat on the terrace of the apartment overlooking the island of Sainte-Marguerite (where the man in the iron mask had been imprisoned), and which was situated at the more glamorous end of the famed Croisette. It was, Smith realised, the first time that he and Gaff had been alone together. Until that point, both had been fed a series of shocking stories about the other. To confound matters, Smith told Gaff that on one recent occasion Despallières had asked him to sign blank pieces of paper. When Smith asked what the purpose of the exercise was, Despallières had answered with two questions of his own: 'Would you be prepared to commit perjury for a friend? Would you lie in court if it was to help that friend?' Despallières was not best pleased when Smith told him, '"I'm not putting my signature on a piece of paper that is blank" – that's what I said to him, and his response was to say I was being silly and with a sulk he went away.'

Having benefitted from Gaff's kindness, Smith took this point in the conversation to thank him for paying the rent due on his London flat when he was jobless. 'It is ever so much more appreciated seeing as though you are in a spot of financial difficulty,' he said not realising what a bombshell he had dropped.

As Gaff reeled in disbelief, Smith revealed what he knew. Despallières had told Bilien that Gaff was broke and had engineered the Jersey trip to get hold of Despallières's money. An indignant Gaff marched to his desk and produced bank statements to prove that he was very far from being insolvent, and indeed, it was his money that was supporting Despallières. A startled Smith went on to say that Despallières and Bray were 'an item'. In response, Gaff asked Smith if he was aware that Despallières had had other lovers. At this, a visibly shocked Smith stormed into the bedroom where Bilien was sleeping, to confront him. A fight broke out and Smith came off the worst. He emerged from the bedroom covered in his own blood, and Bilien fled the apartment, taking with him the keys to a Mercedes, which Gaff kept in a garage beneath the block, and Smith's mobile phone.

The police found the car the following day, abandoned at the railway station in Marseilles. The whole incident left a bad taste but had one positive outcome. It was the midnight balcony conversation with Smith that proved to be the turning point in Gaff's belief in the Frenchman with supersonic charm. 'In one horrendous moment I realised what a fool I'd been,' Gaff told me during a late-night phone call, when he confessed about the last vestiges of contact he'd had with the Despallières camp.

After attending to Smith's injuries incurred in the fight at his apartment, Gaff had phoned Despallières and angrily put it to him that he had lied and cheated on a grand scale. Despallières laughed down the phone and asked his benefactor, 'And what are you going to do about it? Get that little solicitor niece of yours down in Wales to sue me?'

• • •

Summoned to Cannes by Gaff soon after that debacle, at his request I set about going through his cheque-book stubs, bank statements and money transfer orders to discover just how much his six-month friendship with Despallières had cost him. It turned out to be more than £300,000.

He had made several £20,000 payments as well as bank transfers for up to £40,000. And all this had gone to a man who claimed to be a billionaire with properties scattered around the world. We were to establish that during this time, the Jersey bankers had paid Despallières more than £3.8 million in settlement of the money Ikin kept in his account with them, and he had celebrated by spending £30,000 on top-of-the-range television sets and sound equipment for the Chelsea home he had acquired. The rest was saved in accounts at the bank which had once employed Mrs Iacurci.

And Despallières hadn't finished with Gaff yet, as events took another strange turn. With extraordinary impudence, Despallières had called the police to complain that Billy Gaff had stolen *his* Mercedes, which Billy kept in London – the car which had been registered in the Frenchman's name to allow Gaff to park close to Cheyne Place while he looked after him. Despallières claimed he had paid Gaff £10,000 in cash for the £50,000 vehicle and he had a witness to prove it – a former soldier who worked for a London security firm and whom Despallières said he had hired for his personal protection after receiving threatening hate mail from people who said they were friends of Peter Ikin.

In a sworn statement, the witness later testified that he had met Despallières at a Starbucks on the King's Road some months earlier: 'He seemed to be lonely and looking for a shoulder to cry on after the death of his partner,' he said.

He went on to state that on one occasion – 21 April 2009 – Despallières had told him he was going to buy a car and had invited him back to Cheyne Place to view it. There, he testified under oath that he'd met Billy Gaff and his sister Miriam. Once they'd inspected the car, he'd witnessed Despallières take 'a considerable amount of cash' from a tin box and hand it to Gaff in return for what, he said, had appeared to be the car's registration documents.

Gaff was flabbergasted. He had seen first-hand evidence of Despallières behaving deceptively towards others, but had still never thought it would happen to him.

Thanks to the witness's evidence, it was beginning to look as though Despallières had the law on his side. As a precaution, Gaff had the vehicle garaged under lock and key in the grounds of his house in Wales. But there was worse to come: Gaff was arrested after Bilien claimed to have been assaulted by him during the Cannes fracas several weeks earlier. Ultimately, the police did not pursue the case, and Gaff began an action to have Bilien prosecuted for making a false accusation; it had, after all, caused him a period of serious discomfort and anxiety, but he subsequently dropped his action in order to focus on a different case that was unfolding in the High Court in London.

. . .

In Sydney, meanwhile, the beneficiaries of Ikin's 2002 will began to suspect that the August 2008 will produced by Despallières, which made him Ikin's sole beneficiary, was a forgery. Prepared to take Despallières on in the courts, Gaff now joined forces with them. He offered to finance a High Court action proving that the new will was indeed a fake and that the Australians should inherit as Ikin had stipulated in 2002: 25 per cent to the St Vincent's Curran Foundation (for AIDS research and treatment), 25 per cent to the Starlight Children's Foundation of Australia, 20 per cent to his nephew, Father Gary Perritt, 10 per cent to Brian Flaherty, and smaller bequests to his former secretary, Anne Marie Nicol, his friends David Robinson and Robbie Buchanan, and his goddaughters, Tara Robinson and Alexandre Hearne. Gaff engaged the firm of an old friend, Peter Hughman, to contest the forged will and get back the £300,000-plus he had loaned to the Frenchman. Thus, the wheels of the legal system began to grind.

The Australians were not the first to nurse suspicions about Despallières and Bilien. An issue John Reid had not wanted to raise with Ikin at the time for fear of hurting him was the behaviour of Despallières and Bilien when they'd attended his birthday party shortly after arriving in London. Their unusual behaviour as they 'worked the room' that night had caused raised eyebrows among the 60 guests, and Reid recalls: 'At least ten people came up to me later and said, "Who were those two French hookers?"' One guest, Reid's buddy Paul Northcott, says: 'They were like octopuses; their hands and arms were everywhere.'

During the lunch Peter Ikin had hosted at La Famiglia as a thank-you for Reid's birthday-party invitation, Reid had grown suspicious when his questions to Despallières about his global businesses had failed to elicit any convincing answers. He'd made a careful note of the name of his website and had googled the company when he'd got home. The result was as startling as it was dramatic: the man who boasted of owning huge and very expensive properties around the world had his 'billion-dollar business' based in a small rented apartment in a seedy part of West Hollywood. Next Reid had sent an associate in New York to 15 Central Park West, where Despallières had boasted of his multi-million-dollar apartments: the concierge said he had never heard of Alexandre Despallières and that no one of that name lived in the block.

Reid had thought long and hard about telling Ikin of his discoveries, but had decided that, since his friend had just entered a civil partnership with Despallières, it was not the time to break such news. Besides, he'd reasoned, none of these revelations were enough to definitively disprove any of Despallières's claims, and Ikin would soon find out the truth for himself. Indeed, he was shocked that Ikin had not bothered to make such a simple enquiry when Despallières had turned up with his incredible story all those months earlier.

CHAPTER 9

A WOMAN OF SUBSTANCE

Researching Despallières's past I came across a newspaper article showing that he had been working for a Japanese-owned website called Stickam. The article had been written by the highly regarded journalist Brad Stone and been prominently displayed in no less a publication than the *New York Times*. Stone reported that Despallières had gone to work for the company after a chance meeting with a Stickam executive, 'taking an unpaid consulting role as he negotiated his formal position. He said the site's owner, a six-and-a-half-foot-tall Japanese Internet tycoon named Wataru Takahashi, known as "Mr. T" inside the company, began cultivating him to run the site as president.' According to another Stickam worker – let's call him Martin – Despallières never seemed to do much in the office. However, Mr Takahashi looked so favourably on Despallières that when he said two of his friends would like a job they were each given one, although they had no qualifications for the work and appeared to do even less than him.

It was during this time, Despallières said, that he learned about the company's links to Japanese pornography. Despallières stated that it allowed its 600,000 registered users, some as young as 14, to take part in unfiltered live video chats using their webcams. But having failed to secure a 'satisfactory' contract with Advanced Video Communications, which owned Stickam, Despallières had gone to the *New York Times* to expose the conglomerate's shadier activities: 'They are leaders in pushing porn via a Flash player and streaming porn from the United States to Japan,' the paper quoted him saying.

It was Jérémy Bilien who'd summoned Stone to Stickam's West Coast's offices to investigate Despallières's accusations.

'Despallières was charming,' Stone would later write. 'He could easily pass for a male model, and there's nothing like a French accent to give one an air of worldly sophistication. On that day [of the interview] he wore an expensive-looking suit with an open-collar shirt and a gold Piaget watch.' The Frenchman took the writer to the US Bank Tower, the impressive and 'heavily guarded' office building where Stickam was located on the 72nd floor, to show him where the work was done.

Stone's article, headlined 'Accuser Says Web Site for Teenagers Has X-Rated Link', was published on 11 July 2007, and featured a photograph of Despallières in front of the US Bank Tower, looking proud. One thing *New York Times* readers of the prominent story would not have been familiar with was the

name he was using at the time. Despallières was quoted throughout the article as Alex Becker.

Now where, I wondered, did that name come from?

. . .

It was an old Los Angeles acquaintance – a Hollywood gossip
reporter by profession – who led me to the door of Marcelle
Becker, the woman whose surname Alexandre Despallières had
adopted. And what a story she had to tell.

Like other Beverly Hills widows, Mrs Becker – whose
husband Marti had been a powerful insurance magnate – had
taken to frequenting the Beverly Hills Hotel's popular outdoor
swimming pool, and it was there, in 2002, that the man who ran
the pool introduced her to Alexandre Despallières. It's easy to
imagine how that initial meeting would have gone. He would
have flashed his broad smile and she, in brief but costly swim-
wear, would have returned it. 'Alexandre Despallières,' the
well-spoken Frenchman would have said, extending his hand
before she proffered her own, which he would have grandly
kissed. 'You need building up, young man,' she might have
commented, eyeing his slim physique, before inviting him to
join her for lunch at the cabana she used most days.

Their conversation continued long into the afternoon,
during which a doe-eyed Despallières told her that he was a successful businessman with only one thing missing in his life – he
had no family, he was an orphan. That gave them something in

common: both were lonely. Older she may have been, but Marcelle Becker had lost none of the elegance that had been a hallmark of her youth. A stunning woman who spoke to Despallières in French – also her own native language, for she was born in Casablanca – Mrs Becker was not only a widow but had tragically lost her only stepson.

They met again for lunch the next day, and the day after that. Finally, Despallières said he was going to let her into his big secret: he had HIV and, once it developed, the illness was going to take his life. Holding back tears, Marcelle Becker clutched his hand. How dreadful. Was there anything she could do for him?

She still can't be sure how many days elapsed before he answered her question with a question of his own: would she marry him? To any other couple sat in the sunshine beneath the swaying palms that are the hotel's trademark, it might have seemed the most romantic of moments, but Mrs Becker could only laugh. 'You are', she said, 'far too young to be my husband.'

When his audacious suggestion was batted away he looked downcast, but not for long. She had another idea: 'I could adopt you. You could be my son.'

In the days and weeks that followed, the pair made elaborate arrangements for an event that would change their lives. The widow's adoption of the lonely businessman was fixed for 8 October 2002 – Despallières's 34th birthday. First, however, he said he needed to go to Paris to put his affairs there in order. He asked if he might borrow some of her late husband's jewellery, which he had admired on previous visits to Chez Becker. She was only too pleased to oblige, although the thought of him parading items that had belonged to her distinguished husband momentarily jarred. She became curious about who he was seeing in the French capital – curious enough to hire a private detective in Paris to monitor his movements.

The private eye's surveillance produced a major surprise, for the 'someone special' that Despallières wanted to impress turned out to be the eminent French barrister Olivier Metzner. With a host of celebrity clients under his belt, Metzner would later be voted France's most powerful lawyer by GQ magazine. According to the gumshoe it was at Metzner's home – the address Despallières had given her as his own home address – that Despallières was staying. And from the way they stepped out together, often holding hands, it was clear that Despallières turned to Metzner for more than legal advice, although at this stage there was little Mrs Becker could do with the intelligence.

Metzner, who had never married and proclaimed that he preferred independence to having a partner in his personal life, had built from scratch an incredibly successful legal business, first by defending underdogs and then by adding major corporate clients to his roster. He'd defended Continental Airlines against manslaughter charges after a French investigation concluded that debris from a Continental plane had brought down the Concorde supersonic jet in 2000. And he'd represented Jérôme Kerviel, the man blamed for Société Générale's spectacular $4 billion trading loss. Those and other high-profile cases had made him one of the best-known lawyers in French legal history.

Despallières's stay in Paris was not spent merely engaging in social chit-chat with Olivier: on one occasion, he called Mrs Becker to say he was ill and in hospital.

Carefully laid plans for the adoption ceremony suddenly appeared to be in jeopardy when he implied there was doubt over whether he could return to the US. But there followed a miraculously swift recovery, and he was fit enough to fly back to California for the big occasion. Mrs Becker duly went ahead with the ceremony on Alexandre's 34th birthday, which permitted Despallières to call himself Becker.

The lavish ceremony, attended by a few of the Beverly Hills elite, was filmed by Bilien 'as a keepsake for Alexandre', although – since he could barely believe his luck that Mrs Becker had fallen for his plan – it was also proof that the adoption had really taken place (although there were also plenty of witnesses on film who could prove that it had).

The party moved on to a Beverly Hills restaurant for Mrs Becker's planned celebration, and Bilien's film – subsequently posted by Despallières on Facebook with a scrambled soundtrack – shows the principals dining. Seated at their table was an important friend of Mrs Becker, the eminent California politician Nate Holden, who once stood for the mayoralty of Los Angeles. There's a toast raised by Marcelle Becker to 'new beginnings', and she tells those assembled for the celebration that she 'love[s] and adore[s]' her adopted son. Holden is heard promising to get

Despallières whatever papers he requires for living and working in the US.

Alas, the Becker association would not last for more than a few hours, qualifying the adoption as surely the shortest in the nation's history. As the celebration meal progressed, Becker and her new son stepped outside together for a cigarette break. Despallières told his newly acquired mother that he was incredibly wealthy in his own right, boasting about owning two Bentleys (which he changed to three during the conversation) and a stretch Mercedes for 'low-key' travel. He went on to tell her that he owned a house in Paris and a large apartment in Manhattan.

Shrewdly, Becker judged this too incredible for words and told me that this was the point at which she stopped believing him. Until then, she had fallen hook, line and sinker for his charm, just as Peter Ikin and Billy Gaff would. Despite nagging suspicions, she had loaned him yet more of her late husband's jewellery, including a gold Piaget watch encrusted with diamonds and a pair of Bulgari cufflinks studded with sapphires. He'd also helped himself to her husband's clothing and an expensive suit which had belonged to her late stepson, Christopher – which he subsequently wore at Peter Ikin's funeral and on his trip with Gaff to Jersey to meet the bankers. From Marcelle Becker's home he'd acquired the floor-length mink-lined leather coat he would wear to John Reid's dinner party. For his trips to Paris, he even borrowed a four-piece set of Gucci luggage monogrammed with her late husband's initials.

When he asked her to settle the $48,000 invoice for his and Bilien's two-week stay at the Beverly Hills Hotel, as well as the hospital bill he said he had incurred on his Paris trip, she finally had the measure of the man. 'I told him, "No way," and I didn't pay because I knew he was never in hospital.' When I asked her if it was true that he had asked her during their courtship for $200,000, however, she said, 'Oh, he got more than that in the end. What's more, after the adoption ceremony he said, "Now that you've adopted me I am going to inherit everything you've got. I am, after all, your son, your only son."'

Exasperated, she stepped back inside the restaurant and announced to the startled guests that she was going to have the adoption they had just witnessed annulled without delay.

Few can testify better to Despallières's command of the English language than bilingual Marcelle Becker. In a long telephone call to me from her California home, she described him as 'the biggest crook in France' and his accomplice Jérémy Bilien as being 'even worse than him'.

Determined to investigate the man she had once made her son, she said she also discovered that shortly after the adoption debacle he married a woman. 'She was French or American. I used to speak to her on the phone. Her name is Laetitia . . . oh, it's something like "finger" . . . Nail! That's it: Laetitia Nail.' He married her in Las Vegas.

A lot of Marcelle Becker's comments dovetail perfectly with the testimonies of Billy Gaff, John Reid and many others who have spent time with Despallières. A pattern was emerging and, as I listened to her stories, the real man behind the mask was coming into focus. Then, just when I thought this sordid tale couldn't get any worse, Mrs Becker concluded one conversation with the following revelation: 'Oh, and by the way, did you know he also murdered his parents . . . ?'

. . .

Marcelle Becker said she had been told by Jean-Michel Despallières, the eldest of his two brothers, that Alexandre had poisoned their parents. No sooner had that accusation been levelled than Petra Campbell, the ex-partner of Alexandre's other brother, Marc, posted two explosive documents on the internet, in the form of open letters to Despallières.

In the first, Campbell, a savvy media operator, posed several questions to Alexandre:

> Yet another body shows up in your arms, Alexandre.
> How many is that? Five? And a dog. All rapidly
> cremated so they couldn't be autopsied, bar Peter.
> How many people in a lifetime find themselves
> being there at the dying breath of five people if
> [they] are not a doctor or at war?

She went on to say she had contacted a prominent Kuwaiti friend of hers:

That guy you were with when your father died told us that you used to put medication in your father's mashed potato and soup. Your father was pumped with medication when he went to the American Hospital in Paris – those records can be subpoenaed. Your father strenuously denied taking anything. I was there, remember? And whatever happened to the wealthy woman in the States after you told her a sob story of having no family?

I knew Peter too and he [was] an Australian [like me]. He was an icon in our music industry and highly respected. You have never worked a day in your life. You are nothing more than a con artist, gigolo, a danger to good people. Your brothers may have closed their eyes, but not me. I am not related to you and Marc can't stop me this time.

I put the allegation to Despallières's brothers – that they had closed their eyes – and they denied it.

Campbell concluded the letter she published online with this accusatory paragraph:

I have just seen an explicit letter Peter wrote about your impending death last year. As usual, you had just two weeks left to live and it was your dying

wish to marry him so your 'evil brothers' could not
touch your 'billions'. At the minimum, there is
fraud and you can be certain that unless you prove
us all wrong this time by crying wolf too many
times, you will be forced to undergo medical tests
to see if you really do have inoperable brain
tumours. And it won't be hard to find out about
your supposed billion-dollar companies in Japan
and the US.

If that wasn't enough, Campbell had a more ingenious way of
taunting her ex-husband's brother: in her second open letter to
Despallières, she elicited his help with a novel she said she was
writing. The title of her book was to be *I Know What You Did in
Paris* and its central character was a handsome gay gigolo she
called Xavier, who bordered on the psychopathically insane.
Xavier and his brothers had been raised by their father to believe
that they could rely on their good looks and charm to succeed in
life. To Xavier that meant sleeping with older men for money.

He had visions of grandeur and felt his parents
were suburban nobodies. He began to invent a life
story for himself. He pretended to other people that
his parents were famous noble people. He went to
all the right places to meet all the right people. He
soon learned how to get the money he needed to
[match] the story of his [invented] background.

Older, wealthy men loved his youthful actor looks, his wit, and charm. He stole wads of money from their wallets or, as he was a master forger, from their credit cards. Xavier regularly took his parents to the brink of ruin by withdrawing funds from their credit cards.

Ms Campbell went on to describe how the character in her novel pretended he had AIDS, going to extraordinary lengths to prove he had the illness, but never allowing anyone to meet his doctors.

Xavier went on to 'medicate' a famous French architect from whom he had stolen a lot of money before deciding to wipe out his parents so he could inherit their properties. First, he poisoned his dog – 'his mum overfed it anyway' – watching television as the animal died in another part of the room. His father had to be next, but his first attempt failed when the older man recovered in hospital from an induced coma. He was more successful the second time around, putting 'medication' into his father's soup after they had travelled to the South of France for a holiday.

Next his ancient grandmother had to die – 'in Xavier's arms' – because she cost the family too much in healthcare. Finally, he faked his mother's suicide. 'Even though his brothers knew deep inside that Xavier had killed everyone, they didn't say anything,' the outline of her novel continued. 'Xavier made sure to cremate the bodies before anyone could stop him.'

The character went on to meet a wealthy woman in Mexico, who adopted him. 'I haven't written about the fate of their adopting mother yet, except she meets Xavier's brother in Paris one day.'

Close to the conclusion of her plot, Campbell addressed Despallières thus:

> I haven't written the rest yet but there will probably
> be a conflict with the true heirs who insist that
> Xavier pass an objective medical to see if there
> really are two inoperable cysts on his lungs, and if
> he really is dying as he tells everyone. My guess is
> that Xavier will be charged with fraud . . . The
> problem was Xavier knew his brothers wouldn't say
> anything because they failed to report him the first
> time. But Xavier forgot about the other 'evil' witness.
> What do you think? I'd really like to co-write this
> with you.

• • •

In an episode that dovetails with Campbell's plot, Marcelle Becker had something startling to say about her pool-suitor's habits too. She told me, 'Soon after Alex was served with the adoption annulment papers I believe he tried to kill me. It was Passover Night and Alexandre knew I was going to celebrate it at Mastro's [an upmarket steak restaurant on North Canon Drive]. He knew all about it because he was around when I was making the arrangements prior to the adoption. I was served a cocktail there, which the waiter told me had been sent over by an admirer and I foolishly drank it without giving it much thought. It made me violently ill and I was rushed to hospital where I was kept in intensive care for a week. He had poisoned me.

'Before I left the hospital I got a call from Alexandre. I remember his words very clearly. He said, "Why are you afraid of me? Do you think I put two pills in your drink?" I was astonished. I said, "Is that how you killed your parents?" He didn't answer.

'Those were the last words we ever spoke together. Afterwards he and Bilien went to Las Vegas, and Despallières got married.'

The woman Despallières had married was Laetitia Nail, whom Billy Gaff knew as Sandrine Gaillot and Peter Ikin knew as Meg Sanders – the very woman Despallières had told Ikin he would not have at their civil ceremony in 2008 because he believed she wanted to marry him herself. So, she had already done so in a Las Vegas wedding parlour in the spring of 2003. There seems little doubt Laetitia was captivated by Despallières and became one of his closest confidantes. Despallières's marriage served a practical purpose: he qualified for an American Green Card, which allowed him to work in the US. The marriage was dissolved in Nevada in October 2004.

My enquiries in California resulted in an unexpected communication from the other side of the Atlantic. I received a chilling text message in reply to an enquiring email I had sent to Alexandre Despallières's Paris-based brother, Jean-Michel. In block capitals he wrote that Alexandre was a dangerous person and that he needed to protect himself and his family. His missive concluded that he didn't want to know any more about Alexandre's activities because he no longer considered him a brother.

Two hours later he contacted me again and this time his missive offered some advice – I should be 'careful' and repeating the assertion that he no longer considered Alexandre a brother.

Accused of murder and attempted murder, and of fraud on a grand scale, Alexandre Despallières was clearly a dangerous man. But was he guilty of these crimes, and was he a threat to me?

Things were hotting up.

CHAPTER 10

CASTLE IN THE AIR

As my investigation into Despallières's past continued, he was busily spending Peter Ikin's fortune.

While lawyers in London busied themselves with an impending High Court action to disprove the 2008 will and recover the money Gaff had loaned the Frenchman, Despallières decided he was going to have a summer-long party, and what better setting for it than an English castle. Declaring that he already owned a castle of his own in Scotland but that was 'too far north – and anyway, it's being refurbished', he rented Carr Hall Castle close to the Yorkshire city of Halifax for three months at a cost of £8,000 a week.

And renting the castle was just the start of his spending spree. Before he left Chelsea for Yorkshire, Despallières bought three new Porsches, telling Bilien and Bray that they could each have one, although he registered all three in his own name. He also named himself as the driver on all three insurance policies, even though he did not drive.

Travelling by helicopter, he set off for Carr Hall with Bilien. Bray and Laetitia Nail – whom Despallières described as his US assistant – went on ahead by road. All four seemed pleased with their new surroundings. Set in 12 acres of grounds, Carr Hall is a folly, a copy of a Norman castle complete with battlements and towers with arrow-slit openings and arch-headed windows. It comes with its own lake and an indoor swimming pool. To add to their convenience and comfort, Despallières also sent for his 'investment manager', the former HSBC employee Mirella Iacurci whom he had hired at a salary of £5,000 a month. Another guest was his 'bodyguard' – the man who had witnessed for him the 'sale' by Gaff of his Mercedes.

No sooner had they arrived than Despallières realised he had left something behind. Mrs Iacurci, accompanied by Bilien, was sent back to London to collect two steel boxes he had deposited at the bank. Between them the boxes contained tens of thousands of pounds in many different currencies. Once they were safely lodged at the castle, Despallières tucked them away until someone he wanted to impress came to call – one such visitor was Dr Waters. 'Alex would cover the huge dining table with these massive amounts of cash,' says Mrs Iacurci. 'It was his way of showing that he was an important man. How could anyone with so much money on display in these grand surroundings be anything less than successful?'

Comfortably settled in his grand – if temporary – new home, Despallières proudly displayed pictures of his other properties scattered abroad. There was a photograph of him stood in a marble hallway at the foot of a magnificent double staircase. That, he said, was his mansion in Beverly Hills. And there was another of himself with his mother, although that picture came out only when one of his 'special' guests was visiting. He spent much of his time in front of the television, frequently watching back-to-back recorded episodes of his favourite programme, *Murder, She Wrote*, the crime series starring Angela Lansbury.

In addition to the cash on show, he began distributing large sums of Ikin's money by cheque. He donated £220,550 to the National Trust to help Cliveden House restore their yew maze, another substantial sum to the Conservative Party (after saying he'd met Tony Blair who'd disgusted him by trying to tap him for money for Labour Party funds), and chartered helicopters for his lawyers so that they could travel north in comfort, saving him the bother of making journeys to consult them. When he required Dr Waters's attendance to give him an injection he said he would book a helicopter to fly the physician up from London. However, this only happened once as the doctor did not like the flying machines and would not repeat the exercise.

Soon after they arrived, Despallières gave Bilien £50,000 'shopping money', with which he opened an account at the Halifax branch of Barclays. In addition, he gave Laetitia Nail as much as £500 a day in cash for her 'personal use'.

Did Despallières have an inkling about what lay ahead, regarding the court case? Was he a rich man or an excellent con artist? Was he dying and enjoying his last few precious moments, or was he faking his illness and merely enjoying the riches of the battle he was waging – and winning – against Ikin's family and friends?

• • •

On 16 July, representatives from Hughmans legal firm secured an order freezing all the money it was believed Despallières had obtained from the Ikin estate up to that point: £2.5 million. This did nothing to rein in Despallières's free-spending ways.

His visitors included a man he introduced as his 'cousin', one Joakim Giacomoni. He was obviously important because Despallières had him ferried to the castle by helicopter, just like the lawyers and the doctor.

Mirella Iacurci recalls this period: 'So having quit my job with HSBC at Alex's behest I suddenly found myself living in a castle. It sounds wonderful, although at times it was anything but. I witnessed terrible rows between Alex, Jérémy and Laetitia. On one occasion – after he had exhausted the £50,000 "float" – Jérémy asked for some money to go shopping. Instead of giving him cash, Alexandre handed him his credit card together with the PIN. When Laetitia found out she went berserk, even though she herself had access to both the card and its PIN. She and Alexandre rowed for two days over that. It was awful being under the same roof.

'I quite liked Jérémy and would often go with him on his shopping trips, even though I was aware that he shouldn't have been at the wheel of the Porsche because he was rarely, if ever, sober. Alex was happy to have me there partly because I took care of Jérémy, so that was one less thing Alex had to worry about. Jérémy confided in me. He was head-over-heels in love with this guy Paul Smith and wanted Alex to buy them somewhere to live, but Alex said he didn't trust Smith and he wouldn't part with a penny, despite Jérémy telling him that he was entitled to a share [of Peter Ikin's estate].'

From Mirella we also get some insight into Laetitia, who remains an enigma through the whole sorry tale. We know she has three identities and was one of Despallières's confidantes. But Mirella emerged from the fiasco doubting her honesty.

'Initially she seemed okay but when I started working with Alex and going to Cheyne Place, I could see she was not one to trust.' Mirella told me about a time when Despallières had asked for a company to come and clean the flat: '[Laetitia] had arranged it, and they wanted £500 as payment for the work. [Laetitia] was supposed to take care of the payment as Alex was forever giving her cash to pay for things. Anyhow, on that day she told me she was not going to be around to pay the cleaners and she handed me an envelope which she said contained £500 for the cleaner so that I could give it to them once the work was done. I did not think much about it at the time, and I just took the envelope. She left, but when I went to pay the cleaner there was only £450 in envelope, not £500. When I called her and confronted her with this, she denied the mistake and said the correct money was placed in the envelope. Therefore, I paid the £50 out of my own pocket to the cleaner.

'This was just one incident but there were more to come. I could also feel that she resented me a little I think, and was maybe a little jealous when Alex would sit and chat with me. Maybe she saw me as a threat, as Alex was always happy to have me around as he used to say I would make him laugh and enjoyed our chats.'

Mirella told me there were many examples of Laetitia's lying and conniving behaviour. She was, said Iacuri, constantly demanding money from Despallières and asking him to buy a flat for her.

Letters Bilien wrote to Smith from the castle went unposted when Alex discovered them, but Bilien was able to send emails to him, attaching photographs of himself in his new surroundings. The pair had allegedly fallen out over Bilien's failure to secure from Despallières the money for the two of them to buy a house. In one email to car enthusiast Smith he boasted of a new Porsche 911 that he now owned and the castle in which he was living. He concluded his communique with Smith 'I am done with you, I will rebuild myself no matter how long it takes.'

There was a terrifying postscript to their relationship. After enduring weeks of prank calls from Bilien, sometimes on an hourly basis, Smith told me that he was on the receiving end of a house call from his former partner and two 'heavies'. The unsavoury trio managed to enter the building using an old set of keys. Fortunately, Smith had had the foresight to change the lock on the door to his flat, but what could he do to stop them breaking it down?

Sometime later, Smith told me what happened next. 'Jérémy was there, shouting and screaming that the police knew about me, my drug-dealing, my sex-trafficking, my kidnapping . . . Just everything he could think of he said. And he said, "I am going to call the police now." And you know, I just thought to myself, That's not a bad call. You have used your key to get in through the front door and now you are outside, and I don't think you have good intentions. So I called the police and, to their credit, they were there in no time.' Later, Billy Gaff told Smith the goons had been paid £10,000 apiece by Despallières. 'I think I was going to be finished that night if I hadn't changed the locks.'

Smith said, 'Alex was charming, he knew what to say. He had Billy, myself and my friends completely fooled. We were feeling compassionate towards this guy who was having such a hard time with his brain tumour. He always seemed kind and smiling, he played the part well, unfortunately.'

This sentiment was endorsed by Mirella Iacurci: 'Alex told me what I now know to be amazing lies. He was so convincing. He was a very good actor; he would throw fits at the dinner table and somehow manage to turn white in the face while he rolled around on the floor. I often thought he was going to die. My husband and I were due to go on holiday to Hawaii to celebrate our 30th wedding anniversary but Alex persuaded me to cancel it saying how bad I would feel if he died while I was away – that's how persuasive he could be. I never doubted him, I cannot tell you how utterly convincing he was.

'He told me he hated his father because the man had been unfaithful to his mother. It was obvious Laetitia was totally in love with him and would do anything he wanted. He said he didn't like Billy Gaff "because Billy tried to take Peter's place in my life, and no one can ever do that".'

One of Despallières's more startling claims was that his real name was Yonan de Rothschild, a name he could not use because his mother feared that because of the Rothschilds' great wealth he would be kidnapped, just as an uncle had been kidnapped and killed years previously, despite a ransom being paid. Mrs Iacurci continues: 'He'd forgotten that I had his passport with the name Alexandre Despallières in it, but when I mentioned that he said it was the name of a dead man which he had adopted. Incredible as it seemed, it somehow rang true.'

Mrs Iacurci added a note of humour to the information she gave so generously, adding: 'I managed his business affairs totally – I even bought the tins he kept loads and loads of cash in. But I drew the line at accompanying Jérémy when he went to gay nightclubs. "Jérémy," I said to him, "I'm a 50-year-old married woman. I don't do gay clubs."'

· · ·

Despallières found reasons for throwing celebratory parties during his stay in Yorkshire. In August, he announced that it was his 'real' birthday, although that, of course, was not true. His guests at Carr Hall were expected to give him expensive presents to humour him: Nail bought him a watch (although he already had a large collection of very expensive timepieces) and Bilien got him a mobile phone (he had plenty of those too).

Behind the scenes, things remained fractious. The party mood was spoiled for Nail when she received two emails from a mystery correspondent. One read: 'I haven't got anything on you yet, but I will,' and the second: 'I know that you killed your mother . . .' She never told anyone who they were from but suspicion obviously fell on loyal friends of Peter Ikin.

It was not Nail's personal safety that was disturbing Despallières, however. He was getting messages from his lawyers saying that things were not going as well as expected with the High Court battle being fought on his behalf and, of course, they needed more money for their work.

• • •

A little more than halfway through their stay at the castle, and perhaps with the ongoing legal manoeuvres in mind, Despallières announced that he wanted to go back to Paris. Bilien was enjoying himself and made it clear that he not only wanted to stay for the duration but intended to do so. With a rebellion on his hands, Despallières came up with a bizarre solution. He made a will – witnessed by Mrs Iacurci – leaving 85 per cent of his estate to Bilien, 10 per cent to Children in Crisis, and the remaining 5 per cent to the National Trust. His body was to be cremated and his ashes scattered along with those of Peter Ikin, which, on this occasion, he had left behind in Cheyne Place in the cupboard with his collection of pornography. Although the will was made in August, he had it backdated to 9 June in a bid to convince Bilien that this wasn't a reaction to his rebellion but something he had been thinking about for some time. When Despallières was asked by Mrs Iacurci why he was leaving nothing to Nail, he replied, 'I think I've given her enough already.'

Despallières then began to muse aloud about dropping out of the ongoing legal battle for Ikin's money. Having seen the document made in his favour, Bilien earnestly persuaded Despallières not to give up the court fight. It was a move doubtless anticipated by Despallières. 'Alright then,' said Despallières. 'You deal with the lawyers' letters, their constant questioning, and their demands for more money.' Bilien said he would and began responding to the legal emails, but drink got the better of him and he soon abandoned the task.

Despallières's next effort to win his aide back on side was much more dramatic. One evening over dinner, a sombre Despallières said he had decided that the others would be better off without him: 'Things will be better for you if I am no longer around.' A near-hysterical Nail pleaded with him not to do anything to harm himself, but that night Despallières went to his bedroom alone and, before locking the door, told Vincent Bray he must sleep in another room.

The following morning, Despallières had recovered and was chatting amiably with Nail and Bray, offering no explanation of the drama that had taken place.

Finally, it was decided that Despallières and his group would leave the castle on 22 August, taking the two boxes containing what was left of the cash with them. Only Mrs Iacurci was to be left behind to clear up. The night before their departure Despallières, finally bound for Paris, summoned his investment manager and gave her two things: a number that he said was the combination for the safe (which Billy Gaff had bought him) at Cheyne Place, and a list of things he and Nail wanted her to take from the flat and store at her home for him to collect on his return from Paris, 'sooner rather than later'. Then, almost casually, he added, 'And there's some money in the cupboard you should pick up.' When Mrs Iacurci asked him how much money, he was quite specific in his reply: 'About £3 million; Peter was always leaving money about the place.'

Mrs Iacurci was astonished: 'What am I going to do with all that? Where do I hide that sort of money? Do you want me to bank it for you?' Despallières said he was leaving that all up to her but she should be careful when going to the flat to collect it 'as the press and perhaps others are likely to be hanging around there'.

Then she was summoned outside by Nail to share a bottle of wine. A non-drinker, Mirella managed to tip hers into a flower-bed, but not before Nail told her she was going to miss her and then made a point of asking, 'Did he tell you about the money?'

After she had finished clearing up, Mirella was met by her husband and driven back to London in one of the Porsches, which Despallières also wanted her to store. Instead of going straight home, they went to Cheyne Place that night and, conscious of Despallières's warning, did not put on the lights but used a torch to search for the money. In the designated cupboard, they found items including a zipped-up bag containing the urn holding Peter Ikin's ashes, which was stacked on top of a pile of gay porn magazines and films. But no money. Thinking Despallières might have stored the cash in the safe, they tried to open it but the combination number Despallières had given Mirella was wrong. Anxious not to leave such a large amount of cash in the flat, the couple carried the safe out to the car and took it home with them.

The following day Mirella tried to reach Despallières, who was now safely back in Paris, but only Nail was answering her phone, so she told her that the money had not been in the cupboard. There was little reaction. Anxious that they should never be accused of handling money that had perhaps not been honestly obtained, the Iacurcis took the safe into their garden and smashed it open. The only contents were a DVD, a signed first-edition copy of an Oscar Wilde book Despallières had included on the list of items he needed temporarily stored, and £20 in coins. When Mirella did reach Despallières the next day he appeared not to be fazed about the 'missing' money. 'Don't worry about it,' he said. 'Vincent must have moved it.'

So what had the Frenchman sought to gain? Perhaps nothing. It is likely that this was just a further example of his game-playing, and in this instance it was all about appearing rich and powerful. He wanted Mrs Iacurci to believe that he was so rich he couldn't be bothered about a misplaced £3 million, just as he wanted her to believe that he was a Rothschild rather than an ordinary man from an ordinary family. What's more, Nail must have been in on the subterfuge, since she'd asked Mrs Iacurci if he had told her about the money. What money? Both of them knew there was none.

To avoid further stress, Despallières took himself, Bilien and Nail off for a holiday – once again travelling without their benefactor's ashes. Along with Joakim Giacomoni, the castle visitor whom Despallières had introduced as his cousin, the group left the French capital on 2 September for a trip to Milan, where they embarked on an extravagant shopping spree and dined in the city's finest restaurants. For their brief stay the hotel bill came close to £6,000. Giacomoni went in search of somewhere suitable for a longer stay in the city, and from the RentClass agency on Torre di Piazza Velasca he rented an apartment costing €3,500 for a month starting on the second day in September, and naming an address of Metzner's in Orcemont as his own home on the booking form. Bilien had just paid £7,000 of Peter Ikin's money to rent an apartment in Paris via the Le Regent France agency.

The Milan apartment Giacomoni had rented for him did not suit Despallières, however, and after just a few nights there he and his party returned to Paris.

Meanwhile, in London, things were warming up at the High Court. Hughmans' Matthew Jenkins was able to demonstrate that Despallières had in fact so far received in excess of £3.8 million – more than the £2.5 million that had been specified in the original freezing order. While he'd kept quiet about it, the £1.3 million difference had allowed him to carry on spending Ikin's savings. He claimed in an affidavit that he had paid more than £300,000 in wages to Bilien, Bray and Mrs Iacurci.

Accordingly, on 10 September, the Honourable Mr Justice Morgan granted an order increasing the amount already subject to a freezing order from £2.5 million to £3.75 million. Despallières was warned that if he disobeyed the order by spending the money he could be held in contempt of court and was 'liable to imprisonment'. It seemed to have little impact on his travel plans. The following day he, Nail, Bilien and Giacomoni decamped to the Four Seasons Hotel in Geneva. On 15 September, Giacomoni set off for London to deliver to Despallières's solicitor a FedEx envelope containing money which Despallières had been ordered to pay into court, pending a full hearing of the action brought by Gaff and the beneficiaries of Ikin's 2002 will.

Alas, that did not go according to plan either. Despallières's solicitor wrote to him that day, acknowledging the receipt of €108,500 and £6,740 in cash but pointing out that this was approximately £80,000 short of the amount the court had demanded. Warned that this could place him in contempt, Despallières maintained that when the envelope containing the money had left his hands in Geneva, it had contained all the required money but that it was not sealed. When the solicitor had received the envelope, it was. Giacomoni claimed he had left the envelope in a freezer at the Milan apartment and that the maid must have pilfered the contents, but Despallières said that this could not be so because it had all been there when he'd counted it at the Four Seasons in Geneva – 'And anyway, why would a maid only take half?'

Once again it was all a giant game of smoke and mirrors.

CHAPTER 11

A FAMILY FEUD

Life should have been relatively comfortable for journalist Marcel Despallières and his wife, Monique. Neighbours in the Paris suburb where they raised their three sons considered them well off. In addition to their three-bedroom apartment in the Bois-Colombes district, they owned a beachside flat at Le Rayol in the swanky Riviera canton of Saint-Tropez. There was talk of other properties in Levallois-Perret and Corsica, but M. Despallières was not a man given to boasting.

One son, Marc, seemed set for a promising career in banking, and his brother, Jean-Michel, was also destined for a successful future. It was the third son who was the problem. Alexandre always seemed to be in trouble. As a teenager, he showed no inclination to follow a career, and his gains all seemed to be ill gotten. He stole from his father to fund his insatiable appetite for highly expensive baubles and toys.

At least, that's the version of the Despallières family dynamic as presented in an affidavit sworn by Marc's ex-partner of 17 years, Petra Campbell, at the request of counsel acting for the Australian beneficiaries of Peter Ikin's 2002 will in the High Court action instigated by Billy Gaff. She did not mince her words when it came to spelling out exactly what she meant by the insinuations contained in the 'Dear Alex' letters she had posted on the internet.

'Alex has a long history of fraud and theft,' she began. 'I understood from his family that he had a juvenile offender's record in France as well as a police file as an adult.'

The mother of Marc's three children, she seemed in a good position to provide ample description of life in the Despallières household:

> When I lived with Marc I was often in the family home when the parents were discussing with their two [eldest] sons the latest act of fraud Alex had committed. Alex was always having problems with the law for stealing credit cards, for stealing money and forgery.

Such acts, she said, she witnessed regularly:

> Alex often stole his father's credit cards and forged his signature. Often, we went to dinner and the mother would tell us about the level of debt levelled on his father because Alex had spent his money buying designer watches and the latest gold jewellery or some new technological gadget.

> Alex was a master of lies. He lies pathologically
> and took great amusement in seeing just how
> much people would believe the stories he would
> make up.

He was, she said, 'very convincing', reiterating that 'Alex was charismatic, intelligent, and witty. He was good company.'

Presumably aware that this would strike a chord with Peter Ikin's relatives and friends, she said:

> Alex was very popular with wealthy, older
> homosexual men. We were always amazed at how
> much money he was able to extract from these
> men. He would return to his parents' place and
> boast about how he robbed his latest lover of
> 20,000 francs ($5,000), or how his lover had bought
> him clothes or jewellery or computer equipment.

In the 13 years that she lived in Paris as part of the Despallières family, Petra Campbell said she had never known Alexandre to work for a living: 'He appeared to just live off his parents' and other people's money, which he extracted from them one way or another.'

Campbell went on to testify that when he was 16, Alexandre's mother had announced that he had AIDS and was going 'to die very soon'. But expressing, as others have done, a doubt about the true nature of his malady, she added: 'This illness never seemed to manifest itself and I suspected it may have been another of his deceptions.'

Her doubts were expressed in greater detail later in her statement:

> One day, [. . .] in 1996 I believe, Alexandre came home after supposedly undergoing an operation and he said to me, 'I've got a colostomy sac, do you want to see it?' I said, 'Yes.' I do not recall for what purpose he had the sac. By then I didn't believe anything he ever said. He didn't show me the sac then and there. He went to the bathroom first and then asked me to come to the bathroom where he was holding a bag full of faeces. Some months later, he didn't have the sac anymore. I remember seeing Alexandre one day in minimal underwear at his parents' home. I looked everywhere for the scar as I watched him walking around but couldn't see one.

Was this just another game? Perhaps.

Then came the first of her most dramatic revelations:

> Sometime in 1996, I believe, Marc came home in the middle of the day. Marc was working at the French futures exchange. Marc was panicking and near hysterical. He told me words to the effect of

'It's a disaster. My mother has just called to say she is selling all our property and moving to the US with Alexandre.' I asked, 'Why?' Marc told me, 'Alberto Pinto [the celebrated French designer] has filed an accusation against Alexandre for attempting [to] poison [him] and Alexandre is wanted by the police. He will be put in jail and Mum won't let him go to jail. She says he will die in there.'

Upon confronting Despallières, Petra elicited a sort of a confession: 'Alexandre admitted to me that he put something in Pinto's drink and he thought it was funny.'

Preparing to move her life to the United States to protect her son, Mme Despallières was persuaded not to sell up only when Pinto failed to press charges. For Alexandre, the move to America had to wait another day.

If at this point the barristers assembled in the High Court believed that Campbell had spent her finest ammunition, then they were in for a surprise: there was more to come. Much more. She went on to reiterate the accusations made in her 'Dear Alex' letters, suggesting that her partner's brother was already a double murderer and the victims were his own parents. This was certainly no idle accusation and Campbell was no idle accuser: a journalist and filmmaker by profession, she had gone on to be the CEO of International Help Fund Australia, having moved down under with Marc. She had been a media correspondent in Paris, and child-sponsorship coordinator for a German development aid organisation was yet another of her impressive credentials.

Here's how she unfolded the drama:

Marc and I were in Australia when we got the call to inform us that Marcel Despallières, the father of Alex and Marc, had died. I asked his mother, Monique, what had happened. She explained to me on the telephone that Alex, Marcel and Alex's then boyfriend [Bilien], had driven to the South of France. Alex was with Marcel when he died. Marc told me that Alex had already booked the cremation and that no autopsy was done. We got on the next flight to Paris and then Nice as the funeral was to take place in the South of France. We arrived in the South of France just in time to get into our hire car, check into the hotel, and go to the crematorium. The cremation had been rushed through in just a few days.

When we asked Alex how Marcel had died, Alex told us that he invited his father down to the South of France for a holiday. They drove down. Just before arriving at their holiday home, they stopped at a pharmacy and bought some medicine for Marcel. Alex told me, 'I made Papa some soup that night and put his medicine in his soup. I went to check on him at three in the morning to find him dead in his bed.' I asked him, 'What medicine? What did he need, what was he on, what was wrong with him that he needed medicine?' Alex said, 'Just a prescription for stuff.' 'Do you have the prescription?' I asked and he said, 'No, I gave it to the pharmacy.' I asked, 'Why did you go to his room at 3am?' Alex said, 'Because his television was up loud, that's when I found him dead.' Alex was not crying or upset when he told us this story.

Alex's brothers were both convinced that he had killed his father.

As his widow, Monique Despallières inherited her husband's estate, but within a year she would be dead herself.

Marc received a phone call in Australia from Alex to inform him that he had found their mother dead in her bed. When I asked Marc what happened he said that Alex found her lying on her bed with rosary beads in her hands and a suicide note next to her on the bedside table. In the note, she claimed to not [be] able to live without her husband. As before, a swift cremation was organised by Alex within days of the death.

Marc Despallières flew straight to Paris, from where he called his partner to tell her he had read the suicide note.

> He told me the note was too articulate and the spelling too accurate to have been written by his mother. Marc and his brother and friends and myself came to the belief that Alex wrote the letter. Alex had a history of forgery. We were all convinced that Alex had killed her as well.

> During a phone conversation while Marc was in Paris, he told me that he and Jean-Michel had confronted Alex and told him they believed he had murdered their parents. The brothers had a big argument and, according to Marc, Alex threatened to kill them both. Marc told me they made an official complaint to the police that Alex had threatened to kill them but didn't divulge they suspected he killed his parents; just that he had made death threats against them.

For good measure, Campbell added something that no one was going to dispute:

> Marc told me that after the funeral Alex moved to the USA and became a US resident. For a while he apparently resided at the Beverly Hills Hotel in Los

Angeles with a man I understood to be Alex's lover,
Jérémy Bilien.

• • •

Matters finally came to a head at the High Court a fortnight before
Christmas 2009, when Matthew Jenkins presented a scorching
affidavit, which spared no one. The lawyer let it be known that
while Despallières said he was of no fixed abode, he lived with
Olivier Metzner, 'the senior partner in the firm of French lawyers
he has retained to assist him in this matter', at his Paris apartment.
That while Despallières had boasted about his vast wealth to Ikin,
Gaff, Reid and the Jersey bankers, 'he had no money of his own
which can be seen from the accounts before the [Ikin] money
arrived'. That it would be a remarkable coincidence if large payments to his 'so-called employees' were made just a few hours
before he first became aware that a freezing order had been made
against him. That while he let it be believed he had received just
£2.5 million from the estate he knew the true figure was consid-
erably higher. That when he (Jenkins) had tried to reach him at
Carr Hall Castle by telephone, Despallières's mobile had rung out
and gone to answerphone, suggesting that Despallières's claim he
could not get a signal there was untrue. And how was he, a man
who appeared to be 'a vagrant traipsing around Paris', really in
possession of the valuable jewellery he had bought at Cartier as he
claimed? And where were the Porsches?

On 15 December 2009, Mr Justice Arnold overturned
probate of the 2008 will, ruling that the one Peter Ikin had made

in 2002 was the only valid will. This determined that the 2008 version Bilien had brought back from Paris almost a year earlier was indeed a forgery. As the bogus document had been drawn up and witnessed in Paris, any wrongdoing would be a matter for a French criminal court.

Despallières was ordered to hand over most of the money he had received as well as the keys to the Chelsea flat. The three Porsches were to be sold and the money added to the estate, all of which was now going to the Australian beneficiaries after the payment to lawyers on both sides. The money Despallières had extracted from Billy Gaff had to be handed back to him, and as an incentive to return Billy's cufflinks, Despallières would receive an additional £45,000; otherwise the amount would be £25,000. Jewellery was to be returned to the estate, along with Ikin's ashes, and the National Trust had to give back the £220,550 Despallières had so generously donated to it in the crazy week in which he'd bought the luxury cars and rented a northern castle. The National Trust trustees were not happy: they had already thrown a spectacular lunch in their new donor's honour and spent a considerable sum buying the trees he had chosen to sponsor.

It was, however, an agreed settlement: the Australians had no appetite for a long-drawn-out and even more expensive court battle with Despallières and had settled with him. Under the terms of the agreement, he was allowed to keep £500,000 of his ill-gotten gains.

• • •

In a bid to explain why he had failed to respond to the court's original order, Despallières maintained that in addition to his health problems which made it difficult for him to concentrate, his command of the English language was insufficient when it came to understanding legal documents, although it was to be revealed later that he had written a novel, *Amy Knows*, in fluent English.

The first court case at which Despallières was asked to explain himself was over, but it would not be the last.

CHAPTER 12

LIES, DAMNED LIES

For Gaff and Ikin's family and friends, the High Court judgement meant there was at last something to celebrate. At this point, I paused to take stock. By now it was becoming apparent that throughout his life Despallières had survived by elasticising the truth: he was a weaver of intricate artifice. In fact, he thrived on it. As part of my investigation, I scrutinised as many of his fabrications as I could.

Not only did Despallières claim that Carlos Slim had made him a multi-billionaire by purchasing his internet company, as well as laying on his private airliner to transport him to Mexico for surgery on his 'inoperable' brain tumours, but he convinced hardened businessmen that he was the advisor responsible for convincing Slim that he should buy the *New York Times* to stop a wave of bad publicity.

In fact, he'd never met Slim – the photograph he had shown Brian Flaherty of 'Slim's grandson', was a snap of his sometime boyfriend, Jesus Morfin. Then there was the Sultan of Brunei who, he said, had provided his personal 747 to get him from Slim's home in Mexico to his villa in Spain. He had also made the ludicrous claim that he and the sultan owned London mansions next door to each other in Holland Park and that they had demolished the wall separating the properties to create a large garden in which they held joint barbecues for their friends. There were also boasts of an exotic friendship with a member of a leading Arab family, a prince, who he said had given him a basket of apples inside each of which was a valuable wristwatch. The 'prince' has never been identified.

There was no apartment in Paris, no mansion in Beverly Hills, no apartment – let alone three – on Central Park West in New York. Despallières had once brandished a photograph of himself stood in a marble hallway at the foot of a magnificent double staircase, which he said was his mansion in Beverly Hills. In reality, it was the home of the widow Marcelle Becker.

Perhaps one of his most audacious tricks came about after Ikin travelled to Paris to see Bilien on 7 August 2008, following Bilien's kidney stone operation. At that time, Ikin believed Despallières was in Mexico with 'Meg Sanders', undergoing medical treatment for his tumours. In fact, both were close by in Paris, in hiding until Bilien gave them the all-clear after Ikin had boarded the afternoon train back to London. Furthermore, close examination of the emails 'Meg' sent to Ikin in the months leading up to his death suggest that they were the result of close collaboration between Despallières and Nail: expressions like 'I am/he is lucky to have you in my/his life' were clearly identifiable as Despallières's work, and 'positive thinking' was a phrase frequently used by Nail.

That November, Mrs Iacurci was summoned by Despallières to Paris. She was required to take some of the things she had stored at her home for him to a house on the Sébastien in the Bottin district of the city. The items she conveyed included Marti Becker's mink-lined leather overcoat, the signed first-edition Oscar Wilde book Despallières treasured, and his collection of *Desperate Housewives* DVDs.

Emboldened by the fact that he was now in her debt by three months' salary, she took the opportunity to confront Despallières about one of his false claims: 'I said to him, "Alex, you lied to me about being a Rothschild. You're not anybody, just Alexandre Despallières." He answered by going into another room and returned with two large piles of cash; high-denomination notes in several currencies including a stack of €500 notes. There was just so much money. He looked at me and said, "So I'm just Alex, am I?" It said a lot: displaying someone else's money was his way of proving self-worth.'

Unfortunately for Mrs Iacurci, Despallières did not offer her any of the cash as payment for the wages he owed her: 'Olivier will take care of that,' he told her, referring her to his French lawyer friend, Olivier Metzner. But if Mrs Iacurci had any doubts that her employer had lost his fondness for her then she might have been reassured by an email he sent her on 16 December: 'I want to thank you for always being here for me, I knew the first day that you were my sunshine. I love you, my Mirella. You are in my heart and I miss you so very much. We will be together soon. I miss your jokes, your smiles. I miss being around you. Lots of kisses from your Alex.' This was Alexandre Despallières at his tactical best: expressing love for someone he had wronged and who he knew no longer trusted him.

. . .

Following the annulment by Marcelle Becker of his adoption, and his brief marriage to Laetitia Nail, Despallières had a slew of boyfriends. One who lasted for a while at least was Jesus (also known as Jesse) Morfin, a tall, dark, handsome and youthful-looking actor. After making contact with someone who knew Morfin well I was able to piece together Despallières's movements just before he inveigled his way back into Peter Ikin's life. It was a story laced with deceptions great and small.

Born in Los Angeles of Mexican parents, Morfin recalls meeting Alex 'Becker' on MySpace in 2006, and this time it was Despallières who was the much older partner. Well-spoken and smart, Jesus had the potential to be a teen idol. He recalls his relationship with Despallières like this:

'I was living in LA at the time and he was living in New York. He came to meet me a few months later and we had dinner a couple of times: me, Jérémy, Letty [Laetitia] – or Meg or Sandrine, whichever name you know her by now – and Alex, of course. We just hit it off.'

Despite their obvious connection, Morfin later admitted that he struggled to see Despallières as a long-term partner: 'Due to our age difference I didn't really fall in love with him but I did think of him as a very interesting character. He was always trying to show off his "wealth", claiming he was from a very powerful family.'

Shortly after the pair met, Despallières moved to California, ostensibly to be closer to Morfin. Once there he secured a job in downtown LA working for Stickam, the Japanese web company. He soon managed to get Morfin a job there too, which the then-struggling actor gladly accepted, allowing the couple to spend more time together. There was a storm brewing, however, as Despallières tried to compartmentalise his entourage, even when they all lived under the same roof. 'The second day I met Alex he had quickly warned me to keep our relationship a secret from Jérémy and Letty and, with time, this was killing me,' relates Morfin. And things were only to get worse, as the apparently single new arrival caught Bilien's eye: 'Soon Jérémy fell in love with me and this was causing drama for everyone in the household.'

A short while later Despallières was fired from Stickam following his *New York Times* exposé, and with little reason to stay in LA, he persuaded Morfin to move with him to Paris. Although he had received a $30,000 pay-off from Stickam, he was fast running out of money, so he booked cheap flights back to France via Tahiti. Once back in Paris the duo stayed at the modest home of Bilien's mother and sister, but the two women were deeply suspicious of Despallières and, after a furious row, the couple moved to a flat rented in Morfin's name. Morfin was later to deny that he had asked Despallières to get him an apartment. With 2007 drawing to a close, the deeply religious Morfin told Despallières that he wanted to go home to Mexico to share the Christmas celebrations with his family. This he did, only to return to Paris to discover that Despallières had a new friend, a handsome, highly educated young Frenchman called Aurélien Beaucamp, who had a successful career in the human resources department of a large corporate. The master manipulator kept both men in the dark about their love rival, telling Morfin that Beaucamp was working for him and Beaucamp that Morfin worked in his Los Angeles office. They both believed him. And the falsehoods continued. Despallières convinced Morfin that he was a descendant of the Rothschilds, repeating yet again the ludicrous claim that the family feared kidnappers if he were to use the name.

By early 2008 Despallières had decided he wanted to return to America, but he was having difficulty with the immigration authorities – either, he said, because Marcelle Becker had succeeded through diplomatic channels in getting him banned from the country once he was no longer a 'Becker', or because of the restrictions on AIDS sufferers which existed at that time. According to Morfin, Despallières combed the internet looking for someone who resembled him with the intention of stealing their identity. On one occasion, he managed to briefly get hold of Beaucamp's passport without him knowing, and Morfin remembers him studying the photograph, saying, 'Do you think I look like this? We are, after all, the same height and build.'

Finally, Despallières gave up on the plan, conceding that entering America illegally was too risky a proposition. Then, remembering his friend of yesteryear, Peter Ikin, he switched the destination to Australia, where there was no immigration problem. Morfin – who would now be abandoned by the group – recalls Despallières telling the others about his plan, along with the fact that he knew a wealthy man who lived in Sydney. Having somehow managed to maintain the pretence that he himself possessed a vast fortune, he explained that he could not touch his money in France for fear his brothers would seize it. He then persuaded Beaucamp to pay for three air tickets to transport him, Bilien and Beaucamp to Sydney and to put up the money to rent accommodation there. And that's when he made his move on Ikin, re-introducing himself on the door-step of Ikin's apartment in the Kincoppal building, in Sydney Harbour.

Over the weeks that followed it was Ikin and Beaucamp who were unaware that they were sharing Despallières. When the two men met one day, as Ikin picked Despallières up from where he was staying, Despallières convinced the former music mogul that his fellow Frenchman was a business associate from Paris. It was too close a call, however, and drastic measures were required if he was going to successfully rekindle his romance with the older man. That night Beaucamp passed out after consuming a drink Despallières had prepared for him. The following morning Despallières woke him and said, 'You have to go; you have to leave Australia. Don't you remember last night? You were drunk and you caused a terrible incident. The police were called and they're coming back today to arrest you. You've got to get out of the country right now. I've booked you on a flight to New Zealand. I will join you there tomorrow. Come on, we must get to the airport without delay.'

The dazed and panic-stricken Beaucamp was duly dispatched to Auckland, but on a one-way ticket. Despallières, now deeply re-involved with Ikin, did not follow him or even answer his telephone calls. Finally, desperate to get home to France, Beaucamp went to his bank to withdraw money for his flight, only to be told that his account was empty. The €30,000 he'd saved in it had been drained, he believed by Despallières, who had watched him enter passwords when he worked on the computer. Exhausted and still concerned about returning to Australia, Beaucamp phoned his parents, who accepted a transfer-charge telephone call from him and agreed to send him the money to get home. One of the things he had left behind in Sydney was his computer, which Despallières took to Ikin's apartment and used as his own, and according to my sources the computer was subsequently wanted by the French police for the evidence it may have had stored on it.

Despallières's cavalier attitude to his health problems put many people in danger and gave his lovers plenty of sleepless nights. Like others, Morfin had been enthralled by Despallières. After the Frenchman left for Australia, Morfin became seriously depressed. 'I would wake up in the middle of the night swearing, crying and missing him. I even took a gun to my head and the only reason I'm alive is that it did not go off. I really felt that life without Alex was pointless.'

Morfin sent Despallières a photo of himself 'in my lowest state of mind'. Despallières responded with a message that read: 'Even sad you look fucking gorgeous. I love you.'

But Despallières's game was not yet over, as Morfin went on to explain. 'When I left him, I started to feel better, until I heard he had AIDS; then I got depressed again. I don't know what I'd do if Alex had infected me. Alex never told me he had AIDS. I personally don't believe he [did]. I got tested [and came out clean] because I was having unprotected sex with him. Again, I contemplated killing myself but I realised than no man should hurt another as much as he hurt me. It's not worth the pain.'

Despallières's health continued to swing between extremes, or seemed to at least. Marc Despallières, who saw his younger brother only once after 2000, says this of their last meeting: 'It was [2009] and he was not very pleasant to look at. He was very sick, not in good shape at all.' Marc went on to deny Alexandre's claims that he and Jean-Michel had bullied him as a child, had taken a knife to his paintings, and had had him thrown out of the family home when it had become known that he was HIV positive: 'The tragedy behind his sickness was very hard for my parents to understand. They didn't handle it easily . . . He had a lot of money from Maman [following her death] though.'

Just as Morfin was scared, and Marc Despallières was scarred, others were saddened by the whole scenario. Ikin's close friend Robbie Buchanan believes that it was due to Alex's illness, fabricated or not, that Ikin agreed to take care of him: 'I don't think Peter was besotted by Alex. Peter was a very caring man and I think he genuinely believed all the stories and was ready to be there for Alex who he had known on and off for many years. It was not until Alex and Jérémy finally turned up in London to stay with him there that he began to feel a sort of intrusion into his life. Peter was a single man and for the 30 years that I knew him, this would have been the first time that he committed to this kind of relationship. It was bound to cause him irritation and inconvenience. Peter and I would speak almost every day during this time, and I knew that he was exhausted from all the worry. Alex and Jérémy slept most of the day and stayed up all night. This was another reason for Peter's exhaustion and frustration. I don't think he ever doubted that Alex had HIV but he was beginning to feel unsure about the "close to death" stories.

'I met Alex once many years ago in Paris and once in Sydney with Peter. I never liked or trusted him. As I said, Peter and I have been friends for more than three decades and we could read each other's minds backwards. I know Peter was aware of my dislike for Alex so we did not have in-depth discussions about him.'

What else had Despallières said that was untrue? What of David E. Kelley, the eminent American television producer to whom Despallières said he was close, for whom he had written several episodes of *Boston Legal*, and for whom Peter Ikin was required to leave his own home for several hours so the two men could have a meeting, at the end of which Despallières had a new gold watch? I am obliged to Kelley's lawyer who wrote to me on his behalf to assure me that:

> (1) Mr Kelley is not a friend of Mr Despallières,
> (2) Mr Despallières did not write on any episode of
> *Boston Legal* or any other of Mr Kelley's television
> shows ... (3) Mr Kelley did not meet with
> Mr Despallières in Chelsea in October 2008 (or any-
> where else at any time) and (4) Mr Kelley did not
> give Mr Despallières a gold watch or any other gift.

So that nailed that one. It seemed pointless to ask the producers of *House*, the similarly successful American series starring Hugh Laurie, if Despallières had had any involvement in making that, as he had told Billy Gaff he had. Although he must have seen that inevitably he would one day be caught out in such fantasies, it boosted his standing with the individuals he shared them with at the time. So convincing was he that everyone believed him, and his inventions were so captivating that no one wanted to doubt him.

• • •

In September 2009, Gaff's legal firm secured a statement from one Lawrence Levy, owner of David Lawrence Security (DLS), the company that had employed the bodyguard who'd sworn he'd witnessed Despallières's purchase of Billy Gaff's Mercedes, now a 'stolen' car being sought by the police.

Levy said that the previous June he had received a call from a woman with a French accent, who'd said her name was Sandrine and that a friend of hers wished to engage DLS (details of which she had found on the internet) to retrieve their personal belongings from a flat. Levy and the bodyguard went to Cheyne Place where they met 'Sandrine' and Despallières. They duly got the belongings back and Despallières then hired from DLS the services of the bodyguard at a fee of £270 per 12-hour shift plus expenses, and later on a 24-hour basis. DLS were subsequently informed that all the money they had received from Despallières would have to be returned (by then another £20,000 had changed hands) since it was subject to a freezing injunction imposed by the High Court on 16 July.

Levy's affidavit continues:

On 7 October 2009 I discovered that [the bodyguard] had made a witness statement on behalf of Alex in these proceedings. Moreover, I discovered that [the bodyguard] claimed in that statement to have known Alex since April. In October, I confronted [the bodyguard] about the witness statement but he refused to discuss the matter with me. As a result of [the bodyguard] making a statement without my knowledge as an employee of DLS, I have severed all ties with him and he is no longer an employee.

And that was it. Billy Gaff was informed that his Mercedes was no longer a stolen car.

As 2009 unfolded, there was a growing belief among Ikin's friends that Despallières had murdered Peter Ikin. It seems likely that when Ikin had added exclamation marks to his text message to John Reid on the eve of his departure for Brussels and Paris – 'Now on my way to Brussels and then on to Paris!!' –he had meant business on that final trip. And it was not business Despallières would like: Ikin had indicated to Roger Desmarchelier at the Brussels dinner that he was going to close the joint account the two of them had together and he was not going to tear up his 2002 will as Despallières had begged him to do. And then there was the matter of the bounced $50,000 cheque. It was never going to be a happy reunion.

Within hours of Ikin entering the Hotel Abba, the barman said he saw the pair arguing in the bar as 'the older man was telling the younger man he didn't want him staying at his flat in London anymore when he was on holiday'.

Since Despallières was expecting the flat and the apartment in Sydney to be his and much more besides, the words were likely to have come as a tremendous shock requiring immediate action. Over the next six days there were the ambulance trips to hospital where one witness said Ikin looked 'terrified and mad at the same time', and scenes at the hotel with the management becoming increasingly concerned about this group of guests.

Ikin suffered a prolonged, agonising death while Despallières responded with faux gestures that helped cast himself as the victim.

Despallières had sent text messages to Ikin's former secretary (and a wedding-day witness) Anne Marie Nicol saying that Ikin was in pain and vomiting but refusing medical treatment.

In one text message, he told her: 'Tonight I begged Peter to see a doctor and I asked him to go the hospital but he refused once more.' And then he wrote: 'Help me please, I am in tears. He has been vomiting for 24 hours and it destroys me to see him like this.' And then: 'We went to the hospital against his wishes; they asked him to stay because his life is in danger and he needs a treatment for his liver now. He decided to leave the hospital even though he is aware that he can die during the night.'

Initially, the police were satisfied that the non-French speaking Australian had been shown, and signed, a form in English declaring that he accepted the risk to his life if he discharged himself, but when I was shown the form at Brigade Criminelle HQ, it was in French except for one word: 'death'.

Despallières's message to the secretary continued: 'I am crying, there is nothing I can do. I need help. Please, you have to tell him that this is very serious. I am devastated. He is everything I have. He is my only family, he is my everything.'

Then, according to Despallières, he telephoned Ms Nicol in London and, during the conversation, Ikin swore at her. Swore at her? Peter Ikin was not taken to swearing. In Nicol's words: 'He was a kind, generous and honourable man who only wanted to do good for the people around him.'

So how did the perfectly healthy Peter Ikin die? There was, of course, no chance of having Ikin's body exhumed to have a thorough autopsy carried out because of Despallières's haste in having it cremated at the earliest opportunity. It was John Reid who – with the help of Billy Gaff's solicitor, Matthew Jenkins – discovered that under French law some remains have to be removed from the body and kept for one year following a suspicious death. Reid hired the services of Parisian lawyer Marion Grégoire to make an application to the coroner for a forensic examination of Peter Ikin's vital organs. No friend of Despallières's confidant and lawyer Olivier Metzner, Gregoire was more than happy to take on the case.

It cost Reid €25,000 but it was worth it. 'I remember very clearly the morning I got the toxicology report,' he said. 'It came in the post from Marion and it was in French so I had to read it two or three times to understand it. The word that jumped out at me was "lethal". It said that his organs contained *lethal* levels of paracetamol. I felt sick and I cried as I read that piece of paper over and over again: Peter had been poisoned.'

The toxicology report commissioned by Reid showed that Ikin's blood had exceedingly high levels of paracetamol, 297 μg/ml – levels of between 160 to 387 μg/ml are lethal. Ikin would have died in agony, as the chronic overload of the drug was probably ingested over a period of just four to six days. The report's conclusion was that 'death occurred at a certain point after acute intoxication caused serious damage to the liver'.

The poison was Solpadeine, a drug available over the counter at pharmacies in many countries. Solpadeine is for the short-term relief of severe pain such as migraine or toothache. Each tablet contains paracetamol and codeine phosphate hemihydrate. Taken as prescribed and for short periods, it is safe. Manufacturers report, however, that overdose victims can suffer nausea (such as Despallières told Nicol that Ikin was experiencing), irritability (hence Ikin's uncharacteristic outburst at the hospital) and liver damage (which would account for the extreme pain he was in).

In light of the toxicology report, the French police made it known they were keen to reopen the case of what had become known in newspaper headlines as 'The Mysterious Death of Peter Ikin'. Their response came on 10 November 2009, almost the anniversary of Ikin's death and close to London's High Court hearing when the criminal investigation commenced.

· · ·

Some key bits of evidence were lying as yet undiscovered in a locked tin box. Only later would the contents be revealed. By downloading messages from Ikin's computer, Despallières had found that his partner was nursing suspicions about him, aroused just prior to his sudden departure for Paris to see Metzner. In messages sent to two people, Ikin expressed concerns about the financial arrangements he now had every intention of untangling. Printouts of those emails were among the items that

Despallières kept in the box. 'It is clear from these emails that Peter was growing suspicious about Alexandre,' says Mirella Iacurci, who inspected them.

Among the box's other contents were Ikin's death certificate; an invoice for his cut-price cremation; photographs of Despallières with Metzner; a letter from Bilien to Despallières claiming that Gaff's attack on him in Cannes had taken place only after he'd refused to give Gaff certain information about Despallières's activities; a passionate letter from Bilien to his friend Paul Smith; a sealed envelope addressed to Gaff in Bilien's handwriting; a sworn affidavit signed by Nail stating that her marriage to Despallières had been a mistake and had nothing to do with either of them getting a US work permit; a copy of the will in which Despallières named Bilien as his sole heir; a receipt for an £18,000 charcoal drawing someone had given him as a present; the photograph of him and his mother which had only been displayed when someone he wished to impress came to call . . . and a photocopy of Marcelle Becker's passport, along with photographs of her and the headstone on her late husband's grave.

It was an odd assortment of chattels, most of which were of no special importance. But to Despallières they were a sort of insurance policy. They also brought back memories, which would be invaluable were the egotist ever to write his memoirs. His story, after all, was growing richer by the day.

But the box's most shocking content was a photograph taken by Bilien of Peter Ikin in his open coffin. Beside the casket was a smiling Despallières with his thumbs up.

CHAPTER 13
THE HUNT IS ON

With the investigation conducted by the elite Brigade Criminelle gathering pace, all three suspects – unbeknownst to them – were being kept under surveillance on the streets of Paris. Meanwhile, officers had already begun interviewing anyone who could throw light on the matter of Ikin's death – and that included Despallières's former live-in partner Olivier Metzner, who, they realised, knew more than most about the workings of their prime suspect's mind. But Metzner proved a tricky customer. Anxious to protect his reputation, he did his best to convince them he knew nothing about Despallières's trip to Australia or about Peter Ikin's tragic end.

As the French authorities began to piece their case together they called upon yet more witnesses, and by the beginning of June 2010 the net was closing as the questioning of witnesses intensified. When John Reid travelled to Paris, he was grilled by the detectives for five hours, during which he was asked if Ikin had ever shown suicidal tendencies ('never') or if he took drugs ('not since the eighties').

As his interview reached its conclusion, Reid – never daring to believe that the police would share his belief that Despallières had killed Ikin – asked an officer to confirm that they were pursuing the case of the forged will. Her reply was blunt and to the point: 'No, Mr Reid, this is not a fraud case, this is a murder inquiry. We will be picking up Mr Despallières very soon, though he has no idea of that. He cannot get out of the country. That is all taken care of.'

Beaucamp's Australian experience interested the back-room boys at the Brigade Criminelle as they deepened their enquiries into how and why Despallières, Bilien and Nail had first arrived in Sydney.

Within days, the noose tightened still further. At the passport office on Quai de Gesvres a red flag went up when Bilien attempted to get his passport updated. When his name and date of birth were tapped into the computer, a police warning notice flashed on the screen instructing the operator to contact Philippe Meyer, the *commandant de police* at the Brigade Criminelle at its Paris headquarters immediately.

To avoid spooking Bilien, he was kept talking, with the delay explained as a simple computer problem caused by someone of the same name recently reporting their passport missing. Although he clearly noticed that something was wrong, Bilien calmed down when the issue appeared to resolve itself and he was promised that he would have his renewed passport within ten days

When word reached Meyer of the passport office happening he leaped into action, distributing a warning to all police authorities, including the French border police, and issuing a directive that the suspects must not be allowed to leave the country. When Bilien was allowed to leave the passport office he was followed at a discreet distance, and the police heightened their surveillance on all three. From bugged conversations, the detectives learned that the group were planning a move to the United States. Two or three days later all three maintained telephone silence and Meyer decided it was time for action.

On the day lawyers wired Despallières his £500,000 settlement from Ikin's disputed estate he was arrested, along with Bilien and Nail. Police, who would arrest Bray separately, found them at a bijou hotel on the Rue Monsieur-le-Prince on 8 June, where they had rented a suite. When Meyer and his team of detectives entered the apartment-style accommodation they found Despallières slumped spreadagle in an armchair.

'He was barely coherent, he kept moaning and groaning, and pretending that he was dying,' Meyer told me at the Brigade's headquarters, an impressive fortress of a building on the Quai des Orfèvres, from where the investigation into Princess Diana's death had been conducted. 'He kept that up for two whole days, slurring, "I don't understand, I don't know what you are talking about," every time we asked him something.'

Among possessions the police removed from the hotel rooms was a small suitcase belonging to Despallières which was full of drugs (mainly non-prescription ones) – the same case he'd had on him when Peter Ikin's body was found in the Hotel Abba Montparnasse. He also had a thick book on drugs called *VIDAL*, a dense reference book for French physicians, which he had studied 'from cover to cover' according to Bilien and which earned him the nickname Mr Vidal.

At police headquarters they were held in custody for questioning. Subsequently they were placed under formal investigation: Despallières, Bilien and Nail for murder, forgery and use of forgery, Bray for the charges of forgery and use of forgery. Bilien and Bray (Bilien was the first to crack under interrogation) admitted their parts in forging the will, saying that they had done it under the instruction of Despallières. All denied being involved in foul play.

Although they did not yet have enough evidence to support their case, the police believed that Despallières was a serial killer. 'We believe that he murdered his parents, but it was too long ago and we have no hard evidence,' a senior officer told me. 'We interviewed his brother Jean-Michel, who told us that he had suspicions around the circumstances of his parents' deaths. When he and Marc challenged [Despallières] about their suspicions he threatened to kill them. Jean-Michel reported the death threat to the police at the time but later withdrew the complaint. I have no doubt they were, and still are, genuinely frightened of him.'

When Despallières did begin to utter limited responses to police interrogation, it was only to deny the charges set out against him. He explained that the Solpadeine in Ikin's system was self-administered, and that his late partner had regularly taken large quantities of the drug to curtail the tremors he suffered 'when he was coming down from his drug binges'. He also said that Ikin kept a shelf full of Solpadine at his Chelsea apartment. Under a different line of questioning, when asked why Nail used the name Meg Sanders in her emails to Ikin, Despallières once again blamed the deceased, stating, 'That was Peter's idea. He invented the name Meg Sanders.' Later, he was to claim that Ikin had also invented the story that he, Despallières, had brain tumours: 'I have never had tumours,' he said. 'I don't know why Peter told people that I did.' He failed to explain why Nail, posing as Sanders, had written about his 'tumours' in emails to Ikin, which appeared to have been composed with his connivance – but that was just one of many holes in his story.

Remanding Despallières to the bleak Fresnes Prison on the south side of the city, Judge Anne-Julie Paschal turned down his applications for bail made on the grounds of his alleged poor health, pointing out that the prison authorities could take care of his ailments as well as any outside medical establishment.

It was at this point that my correspondence with Despallières flourished. Prison life was to prove extremely hard for him and he wrote to tell me that he particularly missed his cat, Ratatouille: 'I have heard that she is at Jérémy's mother's place. I am not happy with this because she is nuts and not a very nice woman. I do miss my cat very much!' However, his health did not suffer from deprivation on the prison diet. In his first six months of incarceration, he put on 11 kilos.

As for Laetitia Nail, the police may have suspected that she had a bigger role in the crimes that they were investigating, but she was never charged. This suspicion was also shared by Billy

Gaff. A police source said they suspected she was heavily influenced by an ongoing affection for Despallières. So who exactly was this woman? Under interrogation, she said that she had been raised in Mansfield, Ohio, and was estranged from her father who she now thought to be living in Medina, Ohio.

During what turned out to be an incarceration of several months, it was Bilien who suffered most. As the gravity of the situation dawned on him, he longed to see his sister and his mother, who suffered from hepatitis, but communication with them both had lapsed.

Despallières, on the other hand, had regular visitors, in the form of his new friend Clarisse Debout and the eminent barrister Thierry Herzog, whom he had appointed to act as his legal counsel following a falling-out with Metzner. In letters written to me from his prison cell, Despallières described Herzog as 'a brilliant lawyer and a great man'. But he had good reason to heap praise on the new lawman in his life, for he reckoned he'd been hung out to dry by Metzner and so needed a new ally. In one of his letters to me, he wrote: 'Olivier is no longer my friend. You can ask Clarisse what he did to me because she knows the whole story since she was at his country house when he blackmailed me.' To date, there's been no evidence that Despallières was blackmailed.

And it wasn't just Metzner whom Despallières began to distrust. When Nail and Bilien were released on parole in early 2011, he suspected a conspiracy: 'The reason they have been released', he wrote to me, 'could be because they have made a bargain with Metzner (he is very powerful!). But to be honest with you I have no clue why I am in and they are out. All I know is I will be very picky with my new friends.'

He fretted about the media treatment he was getting, too. Despite strict French privacy laws, newspapers and television reports strongly suggested he was guilty rather than merely accused. He emailed me on 2 April 2011 in a state of some distress, to say that an article had just appeared in *France Soir* accusing him of being a conman and a gigolo. *France Soir* was one of the papers to also intimate that he might have been responsible for the deaths of his parents. In fact, newspapers around the world had been carrying stories ever since they'd become aware of Ikin's death – none more vociferously than those in Australia, France and the UK. The reports made much of Ikin's sudden and unexpected death, the fortune Despallières had benefited from, and the fact that he, Bilien and Nail were subsequently arrested on suspicion of murder. The *Daily Mail*'s 'Was Elton John's rock producer friend murdered by his lover?' headline reflected the typical tenor of the coverage. 'It is very hard to have the press against me; the arrows of the press are just to destroy me,' Despallières said to me. 'It is unfair, very unfair.'

Later, I learned the content of a psychiatric report made about Despallières at the time. Experts described him as 'an egocentric, a shrewd strategist and someone who was absorbed by fantasies about success'. He was, they thought, arrogant and lacked empathy, while relatives thought of him as a 'seductive tyrant'. The report described Despallières as having a narcissistic personality, apparent from his feelings of superiority and his need to keep control of all of his relationships, and it acknowledged that narcissistic individuals might well commit crimes to obtain the money needed to 'shine'. He had high intelligence and an elevated sense of self-worth. Several interrogators at the time noted that he was reluctant to talk about his past or his family.

So, with the odds seemingly stacked against him, how did Despallières secure the services of such an eminent lawyer as Thierry Herzog, who was then President Sarkozy's lawyer? It's notable that Olivier Metzner, the flamboyant legal eagle – who puffed on H. Upmann cigars while being chauffeured through Paris in his latest Jaguar – had drawn Sarkozy into the private prosecution by Françoise Bettencourt Meyers of a photographer who had received hundreds of millions of euros in gifts from her mother, Europe's richest woman, the then L'Oréal heiress Liliane Bettencourt. Acting for Françoise Meyers, Metzner had made public tapes recorded in secret by her butler in which the then 87-year-old heiress discussed gifts of large sums of money she had donated to high-placed French politicians. President Sarkozy, who denied accusations of wrongdoing, was placed under investigation for accepting illegal campaign funds from the heiress towards his 2007 presidential election. That case against him was later dropped.

And this wasn't the first time Metzner had set his sights on France's political elite, for this was something of a class war: a state-school educated farmer's son, Metzner did not always see eye-to-eye with his highborn countrymen.

• • •

A story like Despallières's would never be complete without cocaine rearing its ugly head. Despallières was a habitual user, although he told both the doctors in Paris and the police that it was Ikin who took the drug. He had told a similar story about his father to doctors at the American Hospital where Marcel Despallières had been taken after a failed first attempt on his life. It was, however, to satisfy Alexandre's own cravings that Ikin had had copious quantities of the drug delivered to Cheyne Place right up to and including on the day of the civil ceremony. Brian Flaherty recalls: 'Peter phoned me from London on one occasion shortly before his death and told me it was costing him "thousands a week" to keep Alex in cocaine.' So why did Ikin continue to fund the habit? When Flaherty asked Ikin, he simply explained that it was 'the only thing that's keeping Alex alive'.

The woman who supplied the drug to their Chelsea residence ceased to do so after Ikin's death, and a new dealer was found to replace her – but not before Bilien had tried and failed to tap other potential sources. John Reid says: 'Bilien approached me on one occasion and asked me if I could get him "Charlie" and some sleeping tablets. I was quite disgusted. I said to him, "Sorry, you've come to the wrong person."' He got a similar response from Billy Gaff.

On another occasion, Gaff arrived at Cheyne Place to find that Despallières had laid out a large amount of cocaine. 'He asked me if I would like a line. I told him in no uncertain terms that I didn't do that stuff. The following day he said, "Thank you, Billy, for putting me right about cocaine. I've thrown it all away, given up the habit as a result of your words."' Gaff didn't believe him and was told later that it was to snort cocaine that the Frenchman used to leave the dinner table every night before dessert, saying he was going to the downstairs bathroom to clean his teeth.

So what about Ikin? Was there any truth to the claims that he had been taking the drug just before he died? Gaff doesn't think so: 'Peter used to do it in the old days – everybody in the music business did – but he would make a gram last a fortnight, which is astonishing. I'm sure he hadn't touched it for many years.'

* * *

It has to be said that for a middle-class boy from the suburbs of Paris, Alexandre Despallières surrounded himself with some fascinating people. Many of the characters in this book are larger than life. For example, Mrs Becker – the Beverly Hills widow who was briefly Alexandre Despallières's adoptive mother – had sued American Airlines a few years before she met him, claiming that she and her purebred Maltese dog had been roughed up during a flight from New York to Los Angeles.

She said crew members had kicked her and the 13-year-old pet (perhaps aptly named Dom Perignon) after the 8lb dog, for which she had purchased a first-class window seat, had begun to wander around the cabin.

Neither side disputed that at one point during the flight in 1995, Captain Edwin L. Frost had used the dog's lead to secure Mrs Becker's hands behind her. But the airline said she had consumed a cocktail, red wine and half a sleeping pill before becoming belligerent, and when told to keep Dom Perignon in its Louis Vuitton pet carrier she had 'threatened to kill everyone on board'.

She lost her case.

As for Petra Campbell, she was later to claim that it was Jérémy Bilien who'd accompanied Despallières and his father on that fatal trip to the French Riviera. After Despallières senior's cremation, she alleged that Bilien told her that he suspected Alexandre put medicine in Marcel's soup and mashed potato: 'I remember thinking, Oh my God, he just told me that Alex killed Marcel.'

• • •

I have two lasting impressions from this whole black farce. One is the recollection by Billy Gaff's sister, Miriam, of the day in Wales when Despallières announced that he and his cat just had to go to the coast. When Gaff asked him why the sudden need for such a trip, Despallières grabbed the urn containing Ikin's ashes and said in a babyish voice, 'Because I want to take my Peter for a walk by the seaside with Ratatouille . . .' They duly went. Despallières's coquettish behaviour was typical of him when he wanted the sympathy, or indeed pity, of others. He was to demonstrate later that he cared little for Ikin's ashes, and his apparent love for Ratatouille was perhaps an attempt to show that if he cared so much for a kitten, how could he possibly be a cold-blooded killer?

The other is more chilling. During one of Gaff's police interviews in Paris he was asked by interviewing officers if he knew what had caused the sudden and unexpected death of the mother of Laetitia Nail (whom he then knew as Sandrine Gaillot) while he (Gaff) and Britt Ekland were present at Cheyne Place. 'I told them what Alex had told me: old age. The officer said, "Mr Gaff, you are a man in your late sixties: would you consider yourself old?" I said, "No, certainly not," and the officer said, "Well, Nail's mother was only in her fifties . . ."'

CHAPTER 14

IN LOVING MEMORY

Every year, on the anniversaries of the deaths of his mother and father, Alex Despallières observed a ritual: he dived into the ocean with a bunch of roses which he placed on the seabed, just as he said that he and his two brothers, Jean-Michel and Marc, had done when they'd taken their father's ashes to the watery depths after his funeral.

'It is a beautiful gesture,' Alex told me on one occasion. 'It has helped me overcome my grief, to do something as beautiful as that for my father. I did it last month for the anniversary of his passing and I will do it this month for my mother.'

Alexandre admitted that he was no stranger to death. 'Funerals are painful moments. The pain did not stop after their funerals. No, the pain stays, the sadness surrounds you all the time. The nights are dark and you can't see the sunshine even when the sky is blue. Mourning is a long process; you have to learn to live again, to live without the person you have lost. It takes a lot of time. It took me years, and even after all these years I still miss my parents, so much.

'When I think about it everything seems blurry, just like in a nightmare. I do remember the funerals but my brain sprays fog on those memories. It is like my head is not able to handle this kind of pain. I have like a big shadow helping me to cover the pain.'

Later, he had another anniversary to commemorate – the death in 2008 of Peter Ikin, the man he said he loved and whose legal partner he became one month and two days before Ikin left this world. On the first anniversary, he had placed flowers for him at what had been a favourite spot of theirs. On the second, however, in November 2010, he was unable to observe the ritual since he had been charged with Ikin's murder and was incarcerated inside the nineteenth-century Fresnes Prison. He was also under investigation for the possible killing of those in whose memory he had placed springtime roses in the sea – his mother and father.

Instead, his girlfriend, Clarisse Debout, took flowers to the banks of the Seine where he would have carried them himself had he been free to do so. Just as he had instructed from his prison cell, she watched them float towards the sea.

In a letter to me on 7 June 2011, Despallières wrote of both his sorrow and his bitterness:

I have had a very difficult time, life has been more than unfair with me so now I am trying to enjoy every moment to the most. It is not easy because I have been destroyed by so many people, but I am doing my best to make Clarisse and Noë [his girl-friend's young son] happy. Now I am starting to

have my life back, I am lucky enough to have a wonderful person beside me. I could have been alone; I
could have been destroyed by all those accusations.

Accusations, he said, which were largely baseless. He was, after
all, an innocent man. A victim.

After describing the day he and his brothers spread their
father's ashes at sea, he wrote:

At that time I thought I had two brothers but soon I
understood that I was very alone. My brothers have
been so mean. I think they are both jealous, jealous
because my life was different because I live with a
disease, a disease that for a long time was not well
known, for all the doctors thought that HIV was
AIDS. It is not the case but when as a teenager you
learn about your health thinking that at any time
you could end up like that [with AIDS] . . .

I do miss my family but I learned to live a different
life. When you lose the most important people in your
life, you have to find a reason to fight. I am not fighting
for myself; trust me Chris, if it was only for me I
would be with my parents and Peter. If I was selfish I
would jump, make the big dive in order to be away
from this world, a world in which I am an orphan.

When I was sixteen I travelled, I met some
incredible people. I tried to live just for the moment.

What my brothers never understood was why
people like Olivier [Metzner], Peter and others
were falling for me. To my brothers it was a mystery. More than once, they said to me 'What is it
that those people like about you?' I had the answer.
They liked the fact that I was real, I didn't play
games, my life was all about the truth. When others
had to pretend, I was just me and I think this is why
some awesome persons gave me their trust and love.

I remember the love my parents and I shared. That
was my fortune, it made me feel rich, it was priceless.
My parents loved me and I loved them back. And even
if the whole world says words to the contrary I know
that Peter was happy with me and he made me very
happy. When I sent you the notes Peter sent me, I
marked the subject [of the email] 'Treasure' because
they are so important to me. They show me that I was
the one for him just as he was the one for me. Of
course, we had our ups and downs just like everybody, but we loved each other. We were at the same
level. We laughed at the same things. We understood
each other without the need for words.

This was love.

His letter was one of many he wrote to me daily, from prison
and following his release. As the letters piled up, they detailed
what he no doubt wanted me to believe was a sincere account of

the events that had led him to be accused of terrible crimes committed on those whom he professed to love. When he was at liberty, we continued to exchange emails. What follows is his version of the story, pieced together from my meetings and correspondence with him. It is in some places highly biased and clearly not grounded in fact, but it is his story . . .

* * *

It was in spring 2011 that Despallières first invited me to visit him in Paris. London's High Court hearing was history by then but he still faced charges in France. If Alexandre Despallières was the killer, forger, fraudster and conman *par excellence* the French police were alleging, then no wonder I was ill at ease when I set off from London that April morning.

I had been in Paris a month earlier for a Russian convention organised by people who had helped my research for a biography of Vladimir Putin. I was in the Russian embassy when Despallières's girlfriend, Clarisse Debout, called me to say he would like to meet me while I was in the city. I readily accepted the invitation, though not without a certain amount of trepidation, for his recent letters had become a little too familiar, almost intimate. He'd picked up not only the name of my wife – to whom he regularly sent his warm regards – but also those of our dogs. It was almost as though he had ingratiated himself into my family without ever having met us.

That first meeting had taken place at one of the imposing apartment buildings on the smarter side of the 17th arrondissement, with black metal trellis clinging to faux balconies on buildings that were dreamed up 170 years ago by city planner Baron Haussmann.

From photographs I already knew that Despallières was an astonishingly handsome man and I was able to see that for myself on that first meeting when he opened the door of number 87, greeting me with a firm handshake before beckoning me into a fine marble entrance hall and leading the way up a wide staircase to a spacious flat on the second floor. It smelled of money. Waiting to greet us at the door was an elderly couple whom I assumed to be servants – they didn't speak English and my French is so poor that a proper introduction resulted only in handshakes and polite nods.

Waiting in the spacious drawing room was Clarisse, daughter of the noted French actress and singer Chantal Goya, and the highly successful musician and composer Jean-Jacques Debout. The tall, slim blonde – an accomplished photographer – seemed decidedly nervous, and her English was hardly better than my French. Later we were to be joined by Clarisse's playful seven-year-old son, Noë.

While the elderly couple served coffee and cakes, I studied M. Despallières. I could see what Peter Ikin had meant when he'd made it known that his beau looked even more handsome in his forties than he had at half that age. Impossibly boyish, the angular face with its high cheekbones would have won him a Hollywood contract in the days when mundane actors became stars simply because they were photogenic. Dressed casually in a grey jumper and his trademark jeans, his tall, lean body showed no trace of any weight increase, although he assured me there had been some in recent months. But apart from his good looks, he was also bright, polite and excellent company.

That first meeting did not last long – I had promised my Russian hosts that I would re-join them for dinner. But I also made a promise to Despallières – to return to the city and spend more time with him at the earliest opportunity. I wanted to hear his story – or, perhaps I should say, his side of it.

And that's how I came to be back in Paris on that day in April 2011. Once again, he led the way up that winding staircase to the second-floor apartment where the door was already open and that same smiling elderly couple were waiting to greet me and take my coat. It was only later that I learned that the pair who served coffee and cakes were not servants, but rather the owners of the apartment, Helene and Jean Clement. Mrs Clement was a 71-year-old prison visitor who had spent much time comforting Despallières during his period in Fresnes. In short, they were a kindly, affluent couple who had taken him into their hearts.

Clarisse Debout was elegantly arranged alongside her boyfriend on a splendid couch. I opened my shoulder bag and produced the tools of my trade: a Sony Walkman digital recorder and the necessary MiniDiscs.

Incredibly courteous and utterly charming, Despallières answered my opening questions. He had lost both his parents and now his partner. He had been badly hurt by his two brothers and was, he said, permanently estranged from one. 'Yes, my parents were perfect but growing up here in Paris I felt very alone. I had good feelings with my elder brother, Marc – we chat every night now – but I never had good feelings with Jean-Michel, the eldest. I think he lives in Bali now – there was an age gap between us of six years. I was too young for him.'

'What dreams, what ambitions did you have as a child?' I asked.

'None at all,' he said carefully pouring two cups of coffee – one for me and one for Clarisse. 'My father never tried to instil a career in me. My parents put me in a specialist school. I liked sport because I am left-handed, so I was quite good at tennis.' He had, he said, little interest in theatre or cinema, although, during his time in London, he had been taken by the kindly Mr Gaff to see the musical *Billy Elliot*.

And so it went on. As the afternoon light faded, we talked about families, friends, holidays, the music business and everything in between . . . but one subject had to wait until the evening arrived: the mysterious death of his partner, Peter Ikin.

Although we were meeting face-to-face for only the second time, I began to feel I had known Despallières a long while. In a way I had; after all, it had been more than two years since I'd begun my forensic study of his life, habits and fatal encounters, and the many letters he had written to me from his prison cell and afterwards had offered a good insight into the way he thought – or at least how he wanted to be perceived.

Unlike Despallières, his photographer girlfriend looked drawn and tired. Her lined and somewhat sallow face displayed the suffering she had endured during months of twice-weekly prison visits. She was used to the lifestyle, though, for her problems had not started with Alex Despallières. Her father and mother received 18-month suspended prison sentences in 2007 for tax evasion. Being the daughter of celebrities and the woman in the life of a man accused of murder had taken its toll on Clarisse. It had been Clarisse who had contacted me the previous month informing me of some surprising news – that her boyfriend had been released from Fresnes Prison. Her text message had read: 'Dear Chris . . . Alex is free which is great news. I am very happy. I would love to have dinner with you but I have to take care of Alex . . . if there is anything you want me to transmit to Alex, trust me he will be happy to have some news about you.'

Despallières had walked free from Fresnes Prison on 21 March after the Court of Appeal had decided that his further detention was 'not indispensable to the manifestation of the truth'. The court had considered a new report ordered by President Sarkozy's lawyer, Thierry Herzog, and in it a defence expert had argued that Ikin's death was not after all due to a massive ingestion of Solpadeine as stated in an earlier report, but rather by chronic *use* of the drug, implying it was self-administered. The report had gone on to point out that Ikin could well have been under the influence of alcohol and cocaine, the cocktail of which may also have contributed to his death. It was enough to secure freedom for Despallières, although the charges still hung over his head.

The first day we'd spent together in the French capital had been just a start. In the ensuing days, weeks and months we talked on the telephone and exchanged countless emails as Despallières answered all my questions (although not always as comprehensively as I would have wished) and provided numerous photographs and documents to substantiate many of the points he was keen to make. His responses to the accusations made against him enabled me to build his story of the people and events that had shaped his life – both before and after Peter Ikin became part of it.

There was plenty to question him about. What had happened to the fabulous homes and enormous wealth Ikin and others had believed he possessed? What about the rich and powerful people who were supposed to be his friends but now said they had never met him? How had he managed to survive the close-to-death conditions Meg Sanders had chronicled in her numerous emails to Ikin? Why did Laetitia Nail invent the Meg Sanders guise, and that of Sandrine Gaillot? How had he come by the forged will, which had enabled him to inherit Ikin's millions? Why had he needed to borrow hundreds of thousands of pounds of Billy Gaff's money when he'd had plenty of Ikin's, and supposedly his own, to spend? Was Ikin a drug addict? Was he himself? Did he kill Peter Ikin? Did he poison his parents? Why had he handed his parentage to the widow Becker, and did he try to poison her as she alleges? And how did Olivier Metzner fit into the life of a man who said he had been devoted to Peter Ikin for 20 years?

With these questions bubbling away in my mind, we got down to discussing the serious business of Peter Ikin's death in a bijou hotel not far away from where we were talking . . .

CHAPTER 15

'SO MANY PEOPLE SAY I POISON PEOPLE, IT'S ANNOYING'

Less than three weeks after he and Peter Ikin had tied the proverbial knot, Despallières said he took a taxi from what had become their marital home in Chelsea to St Pancras Station. There he boarded a Eurostar train that whisked him in just 140 minutes to the Gare du Nord in the centre of his native Paris. A further journey of around 60 kilometres to the south-west of the city delivered him to Orcemont, home to less than a thousand souls, the most illustrious of whom was the eminent bachelor lawyer Olivier Metzner.

The splendid home Metzner had established (the seafaring barrister later sold it and bought himself Boëdic, an island off the Brittany coast) there was a testament to the brilliant career he had forged. By mining case files and exploiting legal technicalities, he had sprung clients from jail and succeeded in getting large companies and their executives out of trouble.

Despite having sound computer skills, Metzner considered himself too old to master modern technology and an assistant was required to enter appointments into the crammed diary on his iPhone which he kept at his regal office located in the 7th arrondissement, two blocks from the banks of the Seine.

In court, clad in his black robes and wearing his hallmark horn-rimmed glasses, Metzner delivered Oscar-worthy performances, frequently ending sentences with a smile that suggested he had just won another point. An alarming ability to recall vast amounts of legal doctrine more than compensated for a lacklustre academic career. Even so, when required he would invoke his well-known lack of academic laurels: 'Common sense is all I have,' he said, somewhat coquettishly, in his closing speech for Continental Airlines in the Concorde case. 'How could this little piece of metal bring down this huge airplane?'

On that occasion, 'common sense' failed to prevail and his client was found guilty of involuntary manslaughter of the 113 people who'd lost their lives in the catastrophic accident.

But, showing that he had learned a thing or two from his Calvinist parents who'd lived comfortably from land leased to farmers, Metzner had made a huge financial success of his law practice. In Paris he lived in a spacious apartment on the Quai Voltaire, though the ever-helpful and superbly informed Despallières told me that he had lately moved to even more comfortable accommodation on the Rue du Dragon. At weekends the 'workaholic' was known for hosting strategy sessions for colleagues at his former home on the edge of the Rambouillet forest, providing his guests with the very finest fare including an Haut-Brion, the premier *grand cru* Bordeaux wine, followed by generous quantities of old Armagnac.

And that is where he also entertained his friend Alex.

'Growing up here in Paris, I felt very alone, very separate,' said Despallières as he began to share his story with me in the Clements' apartment. 'When I was 16, I discovered that I was HIV positive. No, it was not from a needle, as Peter would tell people; I met someone who infected me. I thought I was going to die. When that happens at such a young age you have to live your life to the fullest and that's what I set out to do.'

Over the many hours that we spoke, he went on to talk affectionately about his parents, particularly his mother, appearing to dismiss the claims that he was responsible for their deaths: 'My mother was perfect, she had a big heart. Maman was very generous and she loved me very much. My father was a journalist. He was very clever, he read a lot, and I think I shared that passion with him.'

After pausing briefly to hand me a coffee and a piece of cake – which I consumed with some apprehension – Despallières said he'd first met Metzner at a dinner party in Paris in the late 1980s: 'He showed me all the signs that he wanted to have sex with me, but I said, "Back off." It was love at first sight for him, though not for me. But he was nice to me. I was his only friend so he could tell me everything.'

Although Despallières said that he had not initially returned the older man's affections, the pair soon moved in together, living under the same roof in Paris for ten years. Metzner funded their lifestyle, taking his new companion on several holidays: 'He took me to Capri, then to Egypt, then Ibiza and Milan.' They also made frequent visits to America, where they would stay at the Beverly Hills Hotel in Los Angeles, at which Metzner would meet yet another set of interesting clients: 'There were all these people dressed in black coming to see him. I discovered that they were from the Church of Scientology and that Olivier was the Church's attorney.'

Despite the diverse paths their lives had followed, Despallières and Metzner found much in common. For instance, neither man had fond memories of his schooldays: Metzner had been thrown out of two high schools for talking back to teachers, had taken three years longer than most students to pass his baccalaureate exams, and had showed a particular distaste for academia; Despallières's father had sent him to a special school where sport was prioritised above scholarship.

The relationship between the two lost something of its early intensity, though, when Despallières said he received a telephone call from the Swiss entertainment promoter Claude Nobs inviting him to join him in San Francisco. 'Soon after I arrived Claude and I had dinner with his friend Peter Ikin who, I think, was managing director of Warner in Australia. Peter was looking at me in that certain way so Claude said to him, "He is mine."' As seems to have happened often in Despallières's life, after just a brief meeting he had made a very big impression: 'The next day I am walking in the street and I hear someone calling, "Alex, Alex . . ." It was Peter. I think he had fallen in love with me.' The two men exchanged phone numbers and once Ikin had returned to Sydney, they would speak almost every day, although according to Alex, Ikin was the instigator. 'He would say, "Come and live with me," and I would reply, "No, I can't, it's too complicated."'

The two subsequently agreed to meet up in New York, where Ikin introduced Despallières to his old friend Billy Gaff before they went together to see Ikin's chum Elton John in concert. In addition to Nobs, Despallières now had a second suitor who afforded him access to the music world's elite. But the relationship with Ikin was to prove short-lived, with the distance between their respective homes too great. 'Peter and I would meet five times a year and each time I had to travel halfway across the world to meet him in places like Bali and Singapore – never Australia, his homeland, though.' Ever polite and thoroughly charming, Alex paused to consider that last phrase as if it was something that bothered him.

So what happened next? Although they fell out of regular contact, Despallières said Ikin was still very much a fixture in his life throughout the years that followed. 'Peter came to Paris after my father died. At that time I was having to take care of my mum – Peter used to call her "Madam". Mum liked him, everybody liked him. At that point, I was trying to decide what to do with my life. Peter said to me, "Darling, we only have one life."'

The supportive nature of their friendship worked in both directions, and Alex said there were many occasions when he believed his companion to be deeply unhappy. 'When he explained to me the life he had it was obvious he wasn't happy. He had to see certain people, but he wasn't happy seeing them. He preferred to make an excuse, he preferred to be alone. He wanted *me* to be in his life but other people he kept away. I saw Peter cry often; I'm not sure he trusted many people. Not long before he died he drew up a list of people he said I could trust and those I could not.'

Returning to the subject of his father's death in 2001, Alex faced Petra Campbell's allegations head-on: 'He had been ill a few months before with flashes in his eyes. He had laser surgery for that and he needed a break so we went to the Riviera. He had an aneurysm and then he passed away. Oh yes, I know the story put about by Petra, Marc's ex, that I poisoned my father with some medicine, but it's not true. Petra is nuts.

'I know that Petra would have people believe that I was also responsible for my mother's death [in 2002] but that too is untrue. Maman ended her own life by taking some pills. I think a neighbour found her. Yes, I inherited from her but I said I didn't want this money.'

After losing both parents, Alex said he stayed on the Riviera for a little while to think. Realising that he had drifted away from his brothers and had very few true friends, he set out to find new companions. 'On the internet I discovered Jérémy Bilien. His story made me very sad: as a kid, he was put in a home. His father had beaten him and his mother was a little bit nuts; she had tried to commit suicide so I decided I would try and take care of him.' Although the duo hit it off and, as we have seen, Bilien became a key figure in Alex's life, the latter described their friendship as 'a mistake', adding that by helping Bilien he had 'created a monster'.

From the South of France Despallières moved to Los Angeles and lived for a while at the Beverly Hills Hotel. 'Olivier paid,' he said. 'He paid for everything.' It was at the hotel that he made friends with Tetta Agustin, the woman who would later introduce him to Laetitia Nail. 'It was obvious to me from the beginning that Laetitia was a very clever person and we became close friends – even closer when her father died. Having lost my own father, I knew the pain she was going through and I did my best to be there for her and to comfort her.'

Alex himself pointed out that Tetta was not the only woman he met at the Beverly Hills Hotel: 'It's ironic because that is where I also met Marcelle Becker. She was a character. We had lunch together and she fell for me.' The timing of their meeting was everything, for both were lonely and recovering from the loss of loved ones. 'She said, "You are the son I wish I would have." She had lost her stepson, Christopher, and I had recently lost my mother so she told me she wanted to adopt me.' It was a chance for both to start again, to build a new family and to give one another a new lease of life.

'I said that was nice and then I went back to France to see Olivier. While I was in Paris, I spent some time in the American Hospital having a little surgery and Marcelle phoned me there and said, "It's Maman." So I went back to Los Angeles and we had the adoption. There was this politician at the ceremony, Nate Holden, and after it was over he said, "Alex, now we are going to give you a new passport and a Green Card" – it's all recorded on film.'

So what went wrong? Alexandre believed his brother, Jean-Michel, was to blame for intervening via a friend who lived in California. 'I believe that it was this friend who talked to Mrs Becker about me, about HIV and stuff like that. Not that that was the cause of her having the adoption annulled. I think the reason for that was that I just wasn't what she expected, I don't know.' If true, had Jean-Michel's Californian friend helped Becker to see a different side to Alexandre? Perhaps. But in the end, it was Despallières who pulled away from the arrangement: 'I had to run away from Mrs Becker. She's a lonely person, but she drove me nuts. My life was a disaster.'

Indeed, Metzner – who had made some considerable investment himself in Despallières – always warned him to be careful of Mrs Becker. 'I was staying at the Beverly Hills Hotel and Olivier was paying the bill so maybe Mrs Becker had the wrong image.

'After my mother died Olivier paid for everything, he sent me money regularly. I didn't know, as you tell me, that Mrs Becker hired a detective who tracked me to Olivier's home while I was in Paris, but I do know that she called Olivier after the adoption – she speaks fluent French – and said she was my mother and she wanted to know if I had money. Olivier says he told her to piss off. He said to me, "I told you so . . ." That was funny.'

So what of Becker's version of events, and her claim that during the celebration dinner following the adoption ceremony the two of them stepped outside and he told her that now he was her son he would inherit her fortune when she died? 'Oh my God, that's not true,' he said, clearly irritated by the question.

And was it true that before she decided to adopt him, he proposed marriage to her? 'Are you crazy? If I wanted to marry someone it was my friend Laetitia.'

And what of her assertion that sometime later he tried to poison her in a restaurant? Despallières offered this response: 'Oh, really? It's all not true. So many people say I poison people, it's annoying . . .'

CHAPTER 16

AND THE BRIDE WORE BLACK

Despite misgivings about his proclaimed business empire, no one doubted that Despallières was a talented innovator. In the run-up to the millennium, he came up with an ingenious idea to reproduce famous French paintings on the back of Métro tickets. He called his project TicketArt and copyrighted it. His friend Thomas Aillagon mentioned it to his father, the politician Jean-Jacques Aillagon, who had been tasked with finding ideas to mark the millennium's arrival.

Impressed by the idea, Aillagon senior introduced Despallières into high political circles, even taking him to meet his close friend President Jacques Chirac, with whom he was photographed. However, Despallières fell out with the statesman when, he said, Aillagon gave the press the impression that the Métro ticket idea was his own. Despite the disagreement, while Metzner asked a fellow attorney, Vincent Courcelle-Labrousse, to investigate the legal issue, Despallières grew closer to Aillagon junior.

Thomas Aillagon was evidently a man Despallières could trust, for, after his mother died, he gave his friend power of attorney to act on his behalf while settling the matter of her estate. The process was to prove complicated, however, due to the animosity between Alexandre and his brothers. On one occasion, Thomas apparently warned Alexandre that his brothers had been to see the notary with a person pretending to be him. As Alex related the story, he added, 'The way my brothers acted after our mother passed away made me sick. All they were thinking of was the money.'

It would take Thomas Aillagon three years to sort out Mme Despallières's estate, and in that time he became, according to Despallières, the conduit via which Metzner transferred money to him following his move to California. After an initial stay at the Beverly Hills Hotel, Despallières took a small apartment off the Santa Monica Boulevard in West Hollywood. Metzner paid the rent, and the first Christmas he was there sent him €10,000 via Thomas Aillagon.

'Every month Thomas would pick up my cash from Olivier and send it to me via Western Union. At one point he came to visit me in Los Angeles but my modest dwelling wasn't good enough for the son of Jacques Chirac's sometime best friend, so he stayed at the Beverly Hills Hotel.

'Peter also came to see me in LA and he didn't like the fact that Olivier was paying for everything. He didn't understand why I had gone so far away from home, why I wanted nothing, why I wanted to be away from everything, but that's the way I was for a couple of years after I lost my mother.'

If Despallières thought he had found a substitute for his mother in Marcelle Becker, then he must have been disappointed by the adoption fiasco of 2002. The widow was, however, not the only woman on the block. In spring the following year he took Laetitia Nail to Las Vegas and married her on 16 March. It was a minimal ceremony conducted in the wedding chapel where he'd read that the singer Britney Spears had got married. It cost him $50 and the bride wore black for the occasion. 'I have to be truthful,' Despallières told me. 'We did it in order to get permits, without which we could not remain in the States.' (Senator Holden had obviously withdrawn his promise to fix things after his friend, Mrs Becker, had annulled the adoption.) 'Ultimately the permits didn't do much good for me because I also needed a Green Card to work in the US and to get one of those you needed to have a blood test, which, due to my health problem, I obviously could never have passed.

'On 4 September 2005 I moved to New York staying at the New York Palace [Hotel] on Madison Avenue which is where Peter and I used to stay together when it was the Helmsley Palace. After a few days at the hotel, I took a flat at 1 Lincoln Plaza and Peter came and stayed with me there, even though he was booked into the luxurious Mandarin Hotel overlooking Central Park.

'The following year I returned to LA renting a handsome two-bedroom, two-bathroom executive apartment at 8811 Burton Way for $6,850 a month. A friend of mine had referred me to a friend of his called Scott Flacks who used to work for MySpace and had been made a vice president for marketing at Stickam, a website which had more than half a million registered users. I met Scott at the Beverly Hills Hotel during the Oscars and he went on to introduce me to the Stickam people who offered me a job. I said, "But I am not alone," so they gave Jérémy and Laetitia jobs too. By this time, Jérémy had met a guy called Jesse Morfin and he said he had to have a job there as well. He was very insistent: Scott used to say, "Jesse is Jérémy's new toy – he has many toys." Then when Jérémy had grown tired of him, he said Stickam had to fire him. After a few months there, I fired myself. I had discovered what the company was doing with its money. I have no problem with people using porn websites, though it is not my cup of tea, but I do have a problem with people – especially big companies – who make their money by making porn available to young teenagers.

'I had to expose them: I called the *New York Times* and gave them the story. As the paper reported in a major article, I was deeply concerned about the link with porn. I pointed out that Stickam was owned by a Japanese businessman called Wataru Takahashi who also owned DTI Services, a vast network of websites offering live sex shows over webcam.' As the *New York Times* reported: 'Teenage members log onto the site each night to broadcast their own lives, often from their bedrooms. They put on makeshift talk shows, flirt with other members in video chat rooms, and often, if they are female, field repeated requests to take off their clothes.'

'Needless to say, that was the end of my term as a vice president at Stickam, but it had much to do with making Peter a more permanent fixture in my life. He read the *New York Times* article and was very proud of me – particularly when he read that I had been a vice president at Stickam. So it was during that summer – 2007 – that Peter asked me a number of times to return to Europe and live with him in London. I wanted to but it was complicated: for a start, he was incredibly organised, and his foreign travel was always set in stone many months in advance. He agreed to slow down on his trips and finally to settle in one place – in no way would I have agreed to settle down with him unless it was in one place. Neither of us was getting any younger and we needed somewhere we could call home. Peter's apartment in Cheyne Place in London was ideal. We had agreed to take our time and the forthcoming 20th anniversary of our first meeting was on the horizon anyway. While Peter stayed on the move in accordance with his long-established itinerary, I moved back to the UK, which was good for Jérémy because he was peeing blood and needed expensive hospital treatment which could be had free just across the Channel in France.

'In the spring of 2008 I travelled to Sydney at Peter's invitation. He had said [on the phone], "Let's meet again, let's start afresh." Jérémy came too, bringing a friend called Aurélien Beaucamp who we had met in Paris. Laetitia followed a few weeks later. I had two and a half weeks to pass before Peter was due back from a trip – to Nassau, I think – and I stayed with my friends in an apartment hotel, a bijou hotel. I wanted to do the tourist thing, to discover the city, it was beautiful. Even after Peter returned, I did not stay with him. He was mad about that, he was mean to me because of my decision. I went to see him in the evenings and he would be drunk. "Why don't you move in with me?" he would say and I would reply, "Because I'm not ready." Anyway, he proposed to me and I said I would think about it.

'On the night of the 20th anniversary we went to this very nice restaurant for dinner and that's where he formally proposed that we should commit ourselves to each other. On the way there he had said to me, "Say that you are living with me," so I had to say to people that I was living with him. It was so many lies that I found it was best to say, "I don't remember," when people asked me questions. I became the "I don't remember" person. When people asked me questions I was playing stupid – he had so many stories, you know, so many stories. It was a trust issue with him. People would say to me, "Oh, Peter is my best friend, blah blah . . ." and some of them only saw him once a year for a few days. Peter was very, very alone; alone in Flat F and alone when he was travelling from country to country to escape tax. It was a similar story with Billy [Gaff], but I think it was harder for Peter because Billy had had a love in his life [Steve Andrews], and although Peter had me in his heart, he had no clue how to catch me. Anyway, I accepted his proposal over dinner and moved into his apartment that night. Then the guessing game began: who would be for us and who would be against us . . . ? We had to hide from some people because I knew they disliked me.'

The guessing game did not last long: Peter Ikin left Sydney in haste – he was running out of the limited days he was permitted, for tax reasons, to spend in Australia. Despallières remained at Elizabeth Bay while Jérémy Bilien was treated in hospital for a kidney stone problem. The three then left Sydney and headed for the UK, where they went to stay with a friend of Nail in Haslemere, Surrey. Bilien made several visits to Paris for hospital treatment.

Despallières's side of the story so far left many questions hanging in the air. Not the least of which was why did Ikin and his friends believe that he was close to Carlos Slim who arranged for him to have treatment in Mexico for supposedly inoperable brain tumours? To make sure I got the point he repeated my question in his answer: 'I don't know why Peter made it known that I was in Mexico as Carlos Slim's guest having brain surgery at that time. I have never been in Mexico, never had brain tumours, never had brain surgery. If Faye [Brian Flaherty] says I told him I had, then that's nice of him. I had shingles around the time I saw Faye.'

Then why had his assistant, 'Meg', gone into great detail in her emails to Ikin – all of which are in my possession – about their time in Mexico and his friendship with Slim? He answered simply: 'I think I once heard [Peter] talking about Carlos Slim . . .' And as for Ikin's assertion that Despallières had written episodes of *Boston Legal* and was a friend of the producer, whom he had entertained at Ikin's London flat, he would say no more than, 'Oh, really?'

And so our conversation went on as afternoon turned into evening. Did he know that Ikin was receiving regular emails from 'Meg'? 'Yes, I've since read a few of those and said, "Okay, I don't want to read any more."' Were they in fact from Laetitia Nail? 'How could I know?' Or could he have written them himself? 'No, they were not my style. Meg was Peter's excuse for people. When Peter passed away, I discovered a lot of things but I said, "No, I don't want to know." What I knew of Peter was enough. I didn't want to know what he was doing on his computer; it was none of my business.

'He would sometimes use a fake Meg to get us out of things. "She" would say, "They can't come/go because Alex is sick." He loved to say I was sick and we couldn't go to things. [For example] it was not long after I moved out of the house in Haslemere to join Peter in Chelsea that John [Reid] invited us to his birthday party, but I had to fight Peter over accepting the invitation. He said, "We can't go." I said, "But I want to go, I haven't seen John in perhaps ten years." I was determined to go because I wanted people to see that I was well and not desperately sick with brain tumours.' Again, he said, "No," and I said, "*You* are sick. We have to go." We went, of course, but he didn't want to stay long and he said to me quite early on, "Let's leave." I said, "No, I'm having a good time." Afterwards he said, "Now we have to take John out to dinner," which we did at the restaurant La Famiglia. John brought Peter Straker. I had Jérémy with me. When I looked at the pictures of that dinner I saw [Peter] looked very sick so I think something was wrong with his health even then.'

In an email, Ikin wrote on 1 September 2008 that he had just spoken to Despallières on the phone and that he had asked him to call his mother who had long since been dead. But when that was put to him, Despallières remained expressionless, insisting he had no idea what Ikin meant by it. So, was Ikin sending the emails to himself? 'No, he's not crazy,' was the response, although he went on to insist that he had no idea who had sent Ikin the emails signed 'Meg'.

He had a more interesting answer for why Ikin had made it known that he, Despallières, owned homes in New York, Paris and Los Angeles: 'He said to me, "People will think you are with me for my money," so he was telling people I had a fortune of my own so they wouldn't think that. As for the multi-million-dollar apartment in New York, I rented a one-bedroom flat on 64th Street. He knew that, he came to stay with me there. When he came to see me in Los Angeles, I was in a small flat in West Hollywood. It was all to stop people saying I was with him for his money. If I had an apartment in Paris, why was I staying in a hotel [where he came to visit and subsequently died]? The only place we had was Olivier's.'

At that point he declared that he and Ikin had stayed together 'many times' at Olivier Metzner's apartment in Paris when the owner was in residence – 'It wasn't a threesome though . . . It was a big apartment. I had my room and Olivier had his.' There was never going to be verbal conflict between his suitors though, because: 'Peter didn't speak French and Olivier didn't speak English.

'Yes, Olivier was in love with me. I loved Peter, and Olivier was in love with me. I think Olivier got jealous when I had my civil partnership with Peter, [because for him] that was the end of "Maybe one day I'll have Alex for me." Olivier wanted me in his life. He had me but I wasn't his!'

What about the wedding? Ikin had said it was a rush job because Despallières had such a short time left to live. 'Look at the pictures, we all look well and happy . . . [the ceremony] was very, very simple; we exchanged cards, we were very happy. We exchanged rings – Peter didn't wear his because he had always worn the same ring, a gold band with a diamond in it, and he didn't want to change that.' Didn't Peter want to know why 'Meg', his sometime correspondent, wasn't there? 'There is no Meg. Meg never existed. I don't know how I can tell you that.

'Look, Peter used to drink a lot, especially when I wasn't there – always wine. There was a problem with his liver, a problem with his heart, and a problem with his lungs – he had a bronchial infection. All things you could die with. He was stubborn, he wouldn't see a doctor, he kept saying, "I'm fine, I'm fine." He was taking pills he got from Bangkok. In the past, he did a lot of cocaine, but he had stopped – not stopped completely, he was doing a little bit just to keep him awake. The last time I saw him do it was in the flat in Chelsea just before I went to Paris to see Olivier [towards the end of October 2008].'

And did Despallières take cocaine himself? 'Just a little, to cheer him up. I take medication [for my illness] and even alcohol is forbidden with it. Anyway, [cocaine] just didn't work for me and the reason I am still in good shape – and I'm 42 years old – is because I never abused drugs and alcohol. I'm not against it; it's just not for me. Peter [tried to encourage me] in the early days, I said, "Peter, I don't like it." He said, "Darling, when people [offer it] to you, you can't always say, 'No, thank you.'" Yes, he did offer it to me. He didn't ask me to drink.'

Despallières denied a suggestion that Ikin was going to confront him in Paris with the news that he wanted to cancel the joint bank account they shared. Instead, he said, they had a discussion before either of them left London about bringing ashore money Ikin held in overseas accounts: 'It was all a part of us being more stable. To have money in Jersey and live somewhere else . . . It was pointless.'

Just days before Ikin's death, Despallières travelled to Paris and Ikin prepared for his trip to Brussels. What, I asked him, happened in those days before they met up again? 'Accompanied by Jérémy I went to Orcemont to join Olivier at his country house, and after a couple of days, [on Tuesday, 4 November, Olivier and I] had a big clash and he kicked me out. His [new] boyfriend Joakim Giacomoni had told me that Olivier had AIDS, so I went to see Olivier in his bedroom and asked him how he was. He said, "I'm fine, I'm fine." I said, "If you are sick . . ." and he said, "I'm fine." I said, "That's not what I heard. Olivier, we are friends, it's been 24 years . . ." And then he asked me to leave.

'I phoned Peter in London and told him what had happened and he asked me to stay in Paris. He said, "It's too late for [you to catch the] Eurostar, my love. Why don't you stay in Paris, because if you come back home tomorrow you will be alone because I have to leave tomorrow for Brussels . . . I will come as soon as possible; I want to spend some days in Paris with you." I think Peter wanted me not to leave France with a bad memory, especially a bad memory caused by Olivier.' Another possible explanation, which I put to him, was that Ikin did not want Despallières in the flat when he wasn't there, but he dismissed that with a mere wave of his carefully manicured hand.

'Anyway, all he had to do was to change his train ticket and make a return from Brussels [via] Paris. So that was the arrangement. Peter was to stay overnight in Brussels and come to Paris on Thursday, 6 November. We were supposed to stay in Paris until Sunday [9 November]. He sent an email to all his friends telling them he would be in Paris for a few days.

'We had that conversation at about nine o'clock at night so an hour later I left Olivier's house and caught a train back into Paris. That was my choice. Joakim said I should stay at the Hotel Abba because it was close to the station where I would arrive and he had a boyfriend called Xavier who knew the hotel because he used to work at Bobino, the cabaret club next door to it.'

Many surprises, but not as many as Despallières was to produce in his account of events in the following days . . .

CHAPTER 17

SO WHAT HAPPENED AT THE HOTEL ABBA?

When the express carrying Peter Ikin from Brussels pulled into the Gare du Nord early in the afternoon of 6 November 2008, it was Jérémy Bilien who was waiting on the platform to greet him. If Ikin was disappointed that Despallières had not come himself to collect him, then he did not show it. Alexandre was waiting at the Hotel Abba, Bilien explained. There, his partner of 27 days was to express some concern about his appearance: 'I think he was ill, a cold, or something like that,' Despallières told me. He had been with the Desmarcheliers in Brussels the previous night and they had had a lot to drink.

'We went to a restaurant – Peter, Jérémy, Laetitia and I – but Peter said he wasn't feeling well and left early [on his own]. He telephoned me about ten minutes later to say he had fallen on the steps of the hotel. I spoke to the hotel manager and said, "What are you doing about it?" He said, "[Peter] is okay," and I said, "No, phone the paramedics." Stupidly, in my opinion, they did not call the paramedics, so I did, but Peter sent them away saying he was fine.

'However, Peter said he had lost a little consciousness and during the night he was puking so I called the paramedics again and this time he was taken to hospital, the Hôpital Cochin. He was mad at me, he didn't want to go, but I had to insist. They sedated him because he wanted to leave and they needed to scan him. He stayed the night and while he was under sedation, they checked everything. When I went to see him the next day, he was in the cardiology department having tests on his heart. During the evening, he was running a high fever and he tore out his IV drip, yelling that he wanted to leave. The doctors told me it was a drug problem, and they couldn't treat it there. They said he used to take pills called Solpadeine, which is codeine and paracetamol and that when you take a lot of codeine it turns into morphine. Instead of taking two Solpadeine he was taking six and he was getting sick.

'He came back to the hotel, still ill with a high fever. I can't be sure whether he went to bed because I went to another room. I was so pissed off he had left the hospital that I changed bedrooms. For the next few days, I begged Peter to see a doctor, but again and again he refused – he always gave the same excuse: "I will be better, I don't need any doctor."

'Day after day he was getting worse, so Jérémy, Laetitia and I walked him to a restaurant – not very far because he was not capable of walking any distance – and I said, "Right, you don't know where we are so you will stay here until you agree to go the hospital." He said, "I want to go back to the hotel." I said,

"No, you are sick, you have to see a doctor, you have to go to the hospital." Again, he refused so I said, "Well, it's simple: you won't find your way back."

'We were only 200 metres from the hotel but he didn't know that, he had no clue. Around 6 or 7pm, he said, "Okay," so I phoned the paramedics. Usually, the paramedics take you to the nearest hospital, which would have been the Cochin again, but Peter wanted to go to a different one, so [the paramedics] were very nice and drove us to the Pitié-Salpêtrière. At the Pitié-Salpêtrière I told them we'd been to the Cochin and they said, "Okay, we'll get his file across." Then, remembering what I had been told at the Cochin, I told them, "He is taking a lot of Solpadeine," and they said, "That's not a problem, we have something for that, for when you take too much. He will be cured in a few hours."

'Then, after they took blood, they told Peter that he needed to stay for treatment but he said, "No, I'm going back to London." They explained to me that if he didn't want to stay they would have to discharge him but I said, "No, this time he has to stay." The doctors were talking to Peter in English. They explained to him the risk of leaving the hospital, but Peter was yelling, "I want to go to my hotel, I want to go to my hotel."

'And that's when I left. I took his false teeth with me, thinking he would never be seen outside without them, but later Jérémy had him discharged. Afterwards Jérémy said that Peter – who Jérémy called Maman – told him that if he didn't arrange his discharge he would never be his son again. So once again, he came back to the hotel.

'We had reservations on the Eurostar back to London the following morning, but Peter had changed his mind. "No," he said, "I don't want to take the train. I don't feel good enough to take the train." I was mad [at him], very mad. I went down to the other room. I was calling everybody to try and get some help. I phoned [his secretary] Anne Marie in London and she said, "It's alright, it will be fine," but I insisted. I said I needed help, that he needed to go back to the hospital. He was taking more Solpadeine at the hotel. The thing is I had no clue, no clue he was taking it. He always carried a little bag with stuff in it.

'I was pissed at Peter. I went back to his room and we had an argument. I told him, "You will just get worse and worse." And with that, I left him for what turned out to be the last time.

'The memory of what followed is particularly painful to me. Someone – and I am not prepared to say who – came to my room and told me to go and check on Peter. I went upstairs to his room but I did not enter it. The door was open and from the doorway, I could see he was lying on the bed. I spoke to him but he didn't answer so I went down to the reception desk and asked them to call the paramedics again. Then the police arrived and the receptionist told them that before I went to his room some-one else had been to check on him – again I will not name that person. The police asked me why I hadn't stayed with Peter when I went up and I told them I didn't want to argue with him anymore, that he was stubborn, that I had taken him twice to hospital to get help from the doctors and that I had called the paramedics several times.

'I said, "I was mad because he got himself discharged from hospital repeatedly, saying he wanted to go back to London, and then the *someone* had told me Peter didn't feel like taking the train in the morning." Now I was turning crazy. I hadn't spent the night with him because I was sick of arguing with him about staying in hospital for treatment. I called his secretary in London more than once, begging for help. I was lost. A doctor gave me an injection, I don't know what it was, but it was to help me relax. I had no idea that Peter was no longer alive, I was in denial.

'As far as I can remember, the police phoned Jérémy sometime later and told him that Peter had had a heart attack and died. When Jérémy told me that, I didn't believe him. I just thought, If we find him a new liver, get him a transplant, he will be alright. Let's find a liver. I went to the Institut Médico-Légal where they do autopsies following deaths that are considered suspicious. They check everything. When I saw Peter, I knew then that he was dead; I was on my knees crying. That is the moment when I realised my Peter was no longer here with me.

'Meanwhile, certain people were making sure that the press would destroy me. Anne Marie was very mean to me, she said, "Stay far away . . ."'

In a message to Jérémy Bilien, sent on 15 November, Ms Nicol said she had received – albeit indirectly – a message from an Australian journalist requesting an interview with Despallières, and being 'wary' of the press she thought that putting anything in print could be 'misconstrued, misquoted, misrepresented, misunderstood', and her advice was that he should 'stay away' from the media.

'Then those people said to the media, "Oh, he burned the body without a proper farewell service and we wanted to make a ceremony."

'I had to go to London because that was where our home was and I needed to get some stuff. At that moment, there was nothing more I could do in Paris. Jérémy was on the phone to Peter's nephew, Father Perritt, and he said the priest had told him that Peter's body should be cremated in Paris. I spoke to Peter's great friend Dolly East, who said she wanted to come from Australia for the cremation. I saw John [Reid] and as far as I remember he said it would be simpler for the cremation to take place in Paris and that he would be there for it, as indeed he was. It wasn't my idea. I was lost, I wanted to die.

'Father Perritt called me and said, "Do you mind if I make a small memorial service in Sydney? We will have a big one later," and I said, "No, go ahead." He wrote me a letter [on 24 November] saying, "Thanks for all you did to arrange the cre- mation for Peter in Paris," and telling me he was going to arrange and conduct a prayer service in Sydney. I think it was Billy who said, "No, they are making an official memorial service there." That made me very angry. I would have gone to Australia for a proper memorial service but at that time I was too sick. They stabbed me in the back and they used the press to do it.'

On 1 December 2008, an email with Despallières's sign-off was sent from Peter Ikin's email on his computer, to every email address he had stored (including Jeeves, the Belgravia laundry), which appeared initially to be an electronic eulogy but which turned into a warning to those who were pointing the finger at Despallières. It read:

> Dear all,
>
> Sorry to disappoint everyone, sorry to have to do this, more sorry than you know but I am against the memorial service organised on 8 December because it is now being presented as the official memorial when it was supposed to be a very small and private affair. Of course, I will be present at the official one with my Peter in my arms.
>
> I hate having to do this and I resent being pushed to it. Peter was my partner, we have 20 years of history and if some of you were not aware of it, that is the way we wanted it. Our personal lives are, for each and every one of us, personal and therefore private. It was our own business and I know I made him happy because he told me so many times. I did not tell him enough how much he made me happy.
>
> Some of you have been wonderful and so support-ive. Billy is here every day and makes sure I am okay and all I can do is to say 'thank you'.

I also want to say thank you to those of you who have sent notes, emails or called - most of you are wonderful and so representative of the amazing group of people Peter had in his life.

Peter had this great ability to always show the positive side, and I know all of you are able to do this as well; it is what we would want. For us to group together, to remember, and laugh . . . not get involved in petty power plays. I know this is a very difficult time for all of you as it is for me. I know how important he was to many of you and I know how certain of you were important to him. I just want everything to be, as he would have expected, liked and insisted things be, meaning with no pettiness, with no gossiping, with friends remembering the best moments with laughter. During our 20 years, we had so much love, and I know each of you had great moments with him. Hold on to those . . . they will not fill the emptiness but they will keep you warm or warmer. It seems like all the lights have gone dim but they haven't. It seems so unfair.

What makes it worse is all the gossip going on. I hear echoes of it and am sure like all echoes it bears no resemblance to how it started out, but still. I find it needlessly hurtful and petty and disappointing from such a group of wonderful people. Oh, I know it is only certain of you; not even the majority. It needs to stop though, because Peter would have hated what is going on in certain quarters right now. So please stop it. Now all I want to hear is how wonderful he is, how he filled your life . . . All I want to hear are good things about Peter because it is all that matters.

Regarding what will be the official memorial ceremony, it will be one where I am present. I will be there with Peter in my arms. I understand everyone wants, needs, to be involved but do not think to organise an official ceremony without me being present. It will not happen, he was my partner.

I seem to have gone on a little but I really felt the need to be quite clear on this. The situation is painful enough as it is. Let us not tarnish his memory, let us celebrate him, remember him, and honour him.

Thank you for your understanding.

Alexandre

When I asked him later to tell me who he had in mind when he wrote of the gossiping, he made the surprising claim that he was not the author of the letter but suggested that his poorly edu-cated assistant might have been: 'Jérémy had taken control of everything. Someone composed an email for me to send to all of Peter's friends. I did copy and paste this email but I didn't write anything. I was devastated. Just to talk about it makes me cry.

'All I know is that nobody killed my Peter. People are mean, very mean. [Subsequently] I went to jail, they took me away from my home, they took everything away from me, but everything was already taken away when I lost my Peter. All those stories about me being a serial killer are ridiculous.

'Did I kill my own father? Of course not. There is a photo-graph of me with Olivier, my mother and my brother Jean-Michel taken six months after my father passed away. If I killed my father, do you think my brother would have been there? I killed no one. I loved my Peter and now I am extremely alone. Thank God Clarisse is with me now, Clarisse and her son, Noë. She was with me when I was in hospital in September 2009, when everybody else was waiting for me to die. Everyone has their own agenda. Well, I wish I could be with Peter because living without him is so painful for me.

'On the day of the cremation I was devastated. I remem-ber seeing John [Reid], Anne Marie [Nicol] and Simon [Burke] there. Afterwards everyone went for a meal. I couldn't eat any-thing, my throat was hurting. I couldn't understand for them. There seemed to be no tears, no sadness for Peter. Afterwards some of them went to do some shopping in Paris.

'It was weird.'

CHAPTER 18

TAKING CARE OF BUSINESS

Once the cremation was over Despallières returned to London and moved back into what had all too briefly been the marital home, Flat F, the apartment in Cheyne Place, Chelsea. 'The place was comfortable,' Despallières told me. 'I tried to improve it. Peter kept nothing of any value there because he let it out during the many months he was not there in order to pay the [council] tax on it.'

It was generally believed that the property, along with Ikin's personal fortune, would become his, as the surviving member of the legal partnership established at Chelsea Old Town Hall on 10 October. However, Billy Gaff – who moved into the flat for a while after making frequent visits – pointed out that Ikin was domiciled in Australia where same-sex marriages were not recognised, and therefore Despallières would probably not inherit his fortune.

And then, in January 2009, a will surfaced, a one-page document seemingly bearing Ikin's signature (and witnessed by Jérémy Bilien and his friend, the journalist Vincent Bray), in which he left everything to Despallières. It was eventually challenged in the High Court: 'They wanted to prove that I forged a will which I didn't,' Despallières told me. 'If I wanted to forge a will it would have been seven pages long like the one [my solicitor] Roberto Germain had drawn up for me in November 2008 in which I left most of my estate to Jérémy and Billy Gaff, not the one-page amateurish thing Jérémy said he collected when he went to Paris. He told me that he saw Olivier and Vincent and then faxed it to my Brighton solicitors that day. There is a note on the fax cover which is in Vincent's handwriting.' The note read, 'Please transmit this document to Roberto Germain as soon as possible. Thank you.'

'When he came back to London Jérémy told me about this will in which Peter had left everything to me. I'm sure he showed it to me. I said, "That's nice of Peter." It was presented to the court in Brighton and was granted probate. I hadn't known the will even existed. Peter and I had made 'gentlemen's agreement' wills before the wedding leaving everything to each other, but they were probably not legal. So yes, we got probate on a single sheet of paper, which was a photocopy. Jérémy was in charge of everything, Jérémy managed everything. Jérémy had told me that he was in Paris with Peter the previous August and that's when the will he witnessed was drawn up. I thought, If Olivier knows about it then it must be the truth.

'Yes, I was generous with the money. I bought three Porsches in one day – I could have bought five. Jérémy kept saying, [*mimics baby voice*] "I want a Porsche, I want a Porsche," so I had to go to the shop, the dealership, and buy him one. Once we were there the salesman said, "Oh, you can have this one too." I was fucked up and I bought three, or was it four? And yes, I bought some Cartier watches. I was so bored I used to go to Cartier almost every day because Peter loved Cartier. I spent hours there.'

But what about the hundreds of thousands of pounds he 'borrowed' from Billy Gaff and resisted repaying? 'Billy was very kind to me, the only one who supported me. I was mean to him because at first I thought he was mean to Jérémy. When Jérémy came back after Billy kindly let him stay for a few days at his apartment in Cannes, he said that Billy had attacked him there. Jérémy was in such bad shape. I trusted him a little bit at first; I said, "Oh my God, what has he done to you?" But I realise Jérémy must have been confused. I got mean with Billy after we had a row about insuring the flat. He had been drinking all day and he was mad at me. I was scared so I locked myself in my bathroom after asking him to leave. 'Cos you know, I'm like a child. I need to take my life in control. It's not true that I asked Billy to leave [the flat] to make room for Vincent Bray. Vincent was Jérémy's boyfriend. Jérémy was in a relationship with Paul Smith who was six years older than him and doing nothing with his life. I thought Vincent was better for Jérémy than Smith. Billy was brilliant for me; he even bought me Ratatouille, my beloved cat.'

Asked why, when he went to Jersey with Gaff, he told the bankers that he had €200 million to deposit, he answered: 'I could have said 300 million. The whole thing was ridiculous, so ridiculous. All these people around me saying, "Just sign the paper." I remember phoning my solicitor in Brighton saying, "Please help me." I was under the influence of pills, which made me do crazy stuff. Nothing bad, just silly – and funny.'

Not long after his move into Cheyne Place, Despallières received emails from people in the UK, America and Australia, variously accusing him of fabricating his illness and – in the case of a New York correspondent – accusing him of murdering Peter Ikin and asking him if he himself 'intended to die anytime soon?' Others were sent by people who called themselves PAI (for Peter Anthony Ikin) and Iris (the nickname some of Ikin's friends called him by). He reported the matter to the Metropolitan Police and contacted the eminent (and decidedly upmarket) Dr Eoin Waters, whose specialist subjects included psychiatry, dermatology and sexual health. Dr Waters wrote a 'To whom it may concern' letter stating that Despallières had been diagnosed with HIV at the age of 17 and listed the treatments he had undergone for the condition. In the letter Waters made a veiled reference to those who had written the accusatory emails, pointing out that his patient's condition had been compounded 'by some acquaintances behaving in an absolutely appalling manner towards Alex' and blamed their 'misguided anger' on their upset at the death of his partner. Ominously, he added that recent blood tests had shown that Despallières's HIV viral load was increasing.

Problems closer to home were troubling Alex further. 'Jérémy was drinking a lot and taking lots of medications. He went into the Priory but he was not getting better. One night he decided to go to the apartment of his boyfriend Paul [Smith], so to make sure he was safe I hired a bodyguard from a firm Laetitia had found online. It turned out to be a good thing Jérémy had a bodyguard because Smith did not want to see him and I think the police were called. Jérémy was very depressed around this time but I don't think it had anything to do with what he had accused Billy of; he had lost his boyfriend, Paul, and he couldn't cope with that.

In a bid to escape from the increasing burden of his problems, Despallières asked Mirella Iacurci – the banker he had hired as his personal accountant – to find him somewhere to spend the summer months. It was, he said, Mrs Iacurci who came up with Carr Hall Castle, close to the Yorkshire city of Halifax. After retaining the services of the bodyguard, he travelled north with the group, which included Mrs Iacurci, Nail and Bilien and a nurse to take care of him. They were joined there on more than one occasion by Metzner's new friend, Joakim Giacomoni, whom Despallières introduced as his cousin. Giacomoni travelled on a diplomatic passport, but according to Despallières this was something he had acquired while working at a place where they produce passports: 'Joakim made one for himself, a diplomatic one.'

During the castle stay, Despallières's condition deteriorated but he denies a report that one night he attempted suicide: 'I had been prescribed Atripla, a medication for HIV, but it was making me very sick. One day I would be okay and the next day very sick. The doctor said I should stop taking it but it was not possible for me to go without medication.'

Medications like Atripla, prescribed for HIV sufferers, stop the virus from multiplying, lower the levels of HIV in the blood, boost the immune system, stop the onset of AIDS, reduce the chances of other people catching the virus, sidestep complications, and increase survival rates.

'Yes, while we were there I did change my will in which I had named Jérémy and Billy as the beneficiaries, and in the new one I made Jérémy the sole beneficiary. He can be very persuasive and at one time, I had thought that Billy had done something awful to him so I changed the will. I gave it to Mirella and her husband witnessed it.' He did not do it because Bilien wanted to go back to France, he insisted: 'On the contrary, he wanted to remain in the UK because that's where his boyfriend was.'

At that point, Giacomoni came up with a plan for the group to leave the UK. 'Joakim had an agenda of his own. His new idea was to get me to go to Milan; he said I needed a break.'

With Bilien, Nail and Vincent Bray in tow, Despallières left the castle on 22 August 2009 and took a train from Leeds on the first leg of their return journey to Paris. Once in France, Despallières divided his time between the residences of Olivier Metzner – the city one on the Quai Voltaire and the country one at Orcemont. Metzner – who at that time was dealing with the legal battle over Ikin's estate – agreed with Giacomoni's idea that his friend and client should go to Milan: 'He said he thought it was a great idea: he said I could rest there, far away from all the problems. He told me not to worry, that Aurélien Hamelle who works with him and spoke fluent English was working with my attorney in the UK and that he [Metzner] was personally overseeing everything.'

In Milan, they stayed briefly at the Park Hyatt until Giacomoni found somewhere they could stay for longer. From the RentClass agency on Torre di Piazza Velasca he rented an apartment costing €3,500 for a month starting on the second day in September and naming Metzner's Orcemont address as his home on the booking form.

When they all met again for dinner in Paris on 19 September, Giacomoni introduced Alex to the woman he was soon describing as 'my angel' – Clarisse Debout. Still trusting his lawyer and not keen to introduce a note of discord into the conversation, Despallières resisted raising the matter of the missing money with Giacomoni but, unknown to him, Giacomoni had already mentioned the issue to Ms Debout the previous evening.

Fast becoming Despallières's closest and most trusted friend – as Laetitia Nail had once been – it was Debout who would maintain a daily vigil by his bedside when, two days later, he was admitted to the Bichat Hospital where he received treatment for his HIV condition over the next ten days. During that stay he learned more about Giacomoni, who had introduced him to her on the evening of Saturday, September 19 and who was now Metzner's boyfriend. 'While I was at the hospital Clarisse came very often, and one evening she asked the doctor if I could go out for dinner and she would bring me back right after. It had been a week I was under the new treatment and the hospital gave permission. We went to a restaurant where we both knew the owner very well. It is Tong Yen, a very famous Chinese restaurant where politicians and artistes go. At the restaurant, she started to talk to me about Joakim. Something had happened between them and she felt she had been betrayed.'

Soon after leaving the hospital, Despallières and Clarisse Debout paid a visit to Metzner's office to discuss not only the case being brought in London but also the doubts they were beginning to feel about Giacomoni. Metzner invited the pair to stay at his country house that weekend and they duly arrived in Orcemont on Saturday, 3 October. Giacomoni was not there and the three chatted amiably over dinner. That night, however, Metzner had a lengthy telephone conversation with Giacomoni, who said he was on his way to join them. When he arrived the following day, the mood in the house changed and after a less-than-happy exchange, Metzner asked his guests to leave.

It was the second time Metzner had kicked Despallières out of his country retreat. What had his former lover done to bring about his expulsion this time? 'When I had been at his office a few days earlier, I shared some concerns I had about Joakim with Olivier. I felt I had to tell Olivier this because he was my friend as well as my attorney but on reflection, I wish I hadn't. I mean, Olivier was in love [with Giacomoni] so I shouldn't have interfered. Even though his first reaction was to thank me, his pride was hurt.'

Before Despallières left, Metzner said something was worrying him: 'He demanded that I return to him all the photographs and papers I had acquired from our times together – we had after all been sharing our lives for more than 20 years. Also, Joakim asked me to hand over all the hotel bills bearing his name but paid by me, as well as the papers I had received from my solicitor.

'They said if I did not do what they asked I would go to prison.'

No sooner had he left Metzner's retreat than Despallières contracted the flu virus H1N1 and was bedridden for more than a week, after which he needed still more treatment at the Bichat Hospital for HIV. Meanwhile, lawyers representing Gaff and the Australian beneficiaries of Ikin's will were growing impatient and demanded proof of his deteriorating condition which had apparently prevented him travelling to London to appear at the High Court and was delaying their proceedings. At this point Despallières consulted another eminent advocate, President Sarkozy's lawyer, Thierry Herzog, a friend of Clarisse Debout's parents, and asked him to take over the work being done by Metzner's associate Aurélien Hamelle.

In London, the legal battle was being waged on Despallières's behalf by his solicitor. Matthew Jenkins (of Hughmans) had been engaged by Billy Gaff to recover the £300,000-plus he had advanced to his late friend's partner, as well as the large sum the Australian beneficiaries were claiming under the terms of the 2002 will.

So, seemingly too ill to travel to London for a legal meeting, Despallières had his solicitor (accompanied by a barrister) fly to Paris to discuss the latest developments. On the first anniversary of Peter Ikin's death, the meeting took place in a small room in Metzner's office suite on Rue de l'Université. Metzner himself remained in his own office throughout, leaving M. Hamelle to take care of the 'close friend' he had so recently expelled from his country home.

Despallières agreed to a final settlement that would require him to return all the money he had gained from Ikin's estate, as well as the dead man's ashes, less £500,000, which he would be allowed to keep in return for bringing to a swift end a legal action that could have dragged on for years.

The person the police had charged as one of his accomplices in the matter of the forged will (and subsequently of Ikin's murder), Bilien, did not take kindly when he received news of the settlement: 'Jérémy was hysterical because I would not tell him the terms,' said Despallières. 'One night I called Clarisse for help. I took her advice and summoned the police. Jérémy was banging on the door and smashing the place up so they arrested him. They kept him in custody for a few hours but when he came back, he was even more hysterical.

'Clarisse put Noë [her son] to bed and came over. Jérémy told her he was going to harm himself unless I told him the details of the settlement. The police had returned and, in front of them, Clarisse yelled at him to stop pressuring me to tell him details of the settlement. She made him hand over all his medicines. As Clarisse says, he is such a drama queen! She was going to Brussels the following day with her mother, and she took Jérémy with them. She even got him a job to try and ensure that I got a rest from him.'

Christmas and New Year came and went virtually unnoticed by the troubled Frenchman, who confined himself to his bed at his flat on Rue Monsieur-le-Prince for most of the holiday period. One action he does remember is opening a bank account. He did this with La Banque Postale (account number 5585864X), giving as his home address the house in Angoville-sur-Ay, Normandy, a property Laetitia Nail had inherited on the death of her mother the previous year.

He was bedbound for most of the following weeks but made a rare excursion from the flat to attend a birthday party for Bilien thrown by Nail at her home. Eleven days later La Banque Postale wrote to Despallières to say it had the pleasure to inform him that his account was now a joint account – in his name and Bilien's. It was a switch he had no recollection of making, although he said it could have been done with his consent when he was under the influence of morphine. 'As you can imagine, with the kind of drugs I was under due to my condition they could have made me do anything.'

Illness or no illness, the stage was set for yet more drama.

CHAPTER 19

NOW IT'S CASTLE FRESNES

Dawn had not yet broken on the morning of 8 June 2010 when the police came to call. Despallières, who had remained behind closed doors for most of the preceding weeks, was barely awake when Commander Meyer and his men made their uninvited entrance into the suite he now rented at the bijou hotel on Rue Monsieur-le-Prince to which Bilien had been followed. Conveniently, Bilien and Nail were also there, making plans for their next move. Following their arrest, they were held in custody for questioning. Subsequently they were placed under formal investigation: Despallières, Bilien and Nail for murder, forgery and use of forgery. Bray for the charges of forgery and use of forgery. Bray was later released on bail while the other three were incarcerated.

'The day the police arrested me I was very sick. I was in pain but they would not allow me to have my painkillers because they said they wanted me to be fully conscious when they questioned me,' Despallières wrote in one letter to me. 'They did not care that I was suffering. My attorney was allowed to see me for just 30 minutes on each of the first two days. He made a report because he said they were treating me like an animal. They obviously thought I was not really ill but my illness is one you cannot fake.

'After being held at a place called Le Dépôt [in Paris], I was on my way to be interviewed by the judge when the police escorting me became concerned and called the paramedics. The judge was informed and she said that I was faking it, but the paramedics said that was not the case and I was rushed to hospital, Hôpital la Santé. There the doctors restored the medication I was on for HIV, which the police had denied me, and they treated me with antibiotics for an infection I had developed. They were nice [in the hospital], they made me eat and I rested. A week later, I was transferred to Fresnes Prison. They were nice to me there too, but each time I had to be transported to the judge's office the journey made me sick and I ended up twice more in hospital.

'The police were very bad to me. During the hours they interviewed me they would not give me anything to eat or drink or [allow me] to use the bathroom. When Clarisse went to see them, they told her that my brothers said I killed everyone but Marc never even went to the police and he was in shock when Clarisse repeated to him what they had told her. They also said that I poisoned [the designer] Alberto Pinto, but when he went to see them he told them that that was not true. Everything was just lies. When they accused me of being a murderer I wasn't scared. I killed nobody.

'I had no idea the police were making an investigation; the police behave extremely mean with me . . . I cannot tell you how mean they were. I told them it's been months since I stepped out of [the apartment]. I couldn't walk; I was in bed 24/7 under morphine, very ill. I had no trip ahead; I couldn't even think of a trip, I was too sick. I don't know why they thought I was going to America, trust me Chris, this was not in my agenda. My days were in bed under medication. They could have tapped my phone – no trip was ahead, I thought I was just going to be hospitalised.'

During his first days in Fresnes Prison, Despallières said he felt an amazing calm. He said he believed he had been drugged up to the time of his arrest and now he was getting clean. He was soon to discover, however, that not for nothing does Fresnes, a medieval institution, have the reputation of being the toughest prison in all France.

'Let me try to give you a picture of how it is at Fresnes,' he wrote to me. 'The place is disgusting, very disgusting.' He went on to describe the cells as being very small, each accommodating three prisoners with beds stacked one on top of the other. 'There was a WC and a small sink.' Because of his medical condition, he was allowed to shower every morning between seven and eight. 'But it is a collective shower for six people at a time . . . It is a place where I had a few bad problems.'

He told me about his cellmates: 'One of them killed his former wife and the second one assaulted his with a knife and hurt her badly. I was so scared to be in a cell with those kind of people.' After a month, he was moved to a cell with two other men who were both in for the lesser crime of drug-dealing.

'Usually when you are charged for murder, they have to put you in a cell with people charged with the same kind of crime. But the administration made an exception [for me]; I did not fit with the profile the police try to give about me. I received many threats and I had some bad experiences . . . I had great treatment from the people working there, because I was not the kind of person yelling, I never banged the door, I was following the rules.' His words took my mind back to the description of him that Billy Gaff's sister, Miriam, had offered: he was the nicest, kindest, most charming man she had ever met.

'The food at Fresnes is not food,' he went on. 'It is something strange, if you dare take the food, you are sick. So you have no other choice than buying your own food. My cell was full of pictures on the walls, pictures that Clarisse sent to me; I was happy because it is rare to have a nice cell and, because of Clarisse, my cell looked good.

'All the people working at Fresnes were very nice with me . . . To be in detention is very hard but they supported me a lot, they helped me a lot. People were insulting me all the time . . . I stayed in my cell because I was the target of a few stupid prisoners. This detention was very hard because of my HIV treatment; being in detention with my kind of treatment is not really compatible.'

How, I had asked him, was he passing his time in purgatory? He said he liked all kinds of music, adding, 'I usually play the radio.' He was also being visited by Clarisse's many friends. He told me about the death of Clarisse's paternal grandmother – a death he could hardly have been accused of causing since the lady was, he assured me, 104 years old.

His one privilege was a television set in his cell, which cost those who were prepared to pay for it €30 a month. Despallières did shell out for it, but regretted doing so when, one night, his face appeared on the screen during a newscast with details of his alleged crimes. 'They were saying that I was a serial killer, that I had killed my family. Oh my gosh, you can imagine what happened to me in the shower the following day and for weeks after . . . It was hell for me; I could not even go out for the twice-daily exercise periods. I was fucked. If it had not been for Clarisse's visits I would have killed myself, hanged myself – that's the only way you can do it.'

The newscast was also watched by Bilien, incarcerated separately in Maison d'Arrêt la Santé. To his annoyance, Despallières learned that Bilien's TV set was funded through his access to their joint account at La Banque Postale. By now, he was growing increasingly angry with his two co-defendants.

He was released after nine months in prison on 23 March 2011 following a successful appeal to the European Court of Human Rights, which had decided that his detention was 'not indispensable to the manifestation of the truth'. Clutching the few belongings he'd had in his possession when he was arrested, he was collected by the understanding Clarisse Debout, and went to stay with her.

Following his release and another meeting with me at the apartment on Rue Ampère, Despallières emailed me daily – up to a dozen times a day. He never refused to answer any of my questions, but on just one occasion, he became seriously rattled at one I put to him. I said his accusers were convinced he had murdered Peter Ikin using Solpadeine. Had he ever bought the medication for him? I asked.

In an uncharacteristically angry reply, he demanded, 'Who are my accusers? Petra Campbell? John Reid?' He went on to claim that five different experts had provided reports in his favour. 'So I don't think that anyone can now possibly think that I killed Peter. Those accusations are very hurting, unpleasant, and defamatory. I have in my possession proof that Peter loved me.' He went on to insist that Father Perritt had been aware of his intention to have Ikin's body cremated. 'This whole story is just ridiculous. I've been very patient, I waited, I said nothing, but now it is time for me to speak . . . People are saying that I killed my parents and that I cremated them. What the hell? I did not cremate them . . . Jean-Michel cremated my mother and I have a copy of the certificate. So please don't get fooled by people.

'I told you I have many documents, and not just some copy – original documents. They started a war, they didn't win. Yes, they succeeded to put me to jail, but trust me Chris; they will have to respond to their actions, you cannot simply say, "He killed everyone." NO, NO, NO, I killed no one. I brought Peter to the hospital twice, I told them about the Sol-padeine, they were more than aware that Peter was addicted to many kind of drugs. He is not dead because he took too much Solpadeine; he was abusing substances since a while. Those are facts, Chris.

'I did not discharge Peter from Salpêtrière; I asked for help and nobody was kind enough to help me. The messages from Anne Marie Nicol on my phone are unbelievable. She just said, "He will be fine, nothing to worry about, Peter is like that, he hates doctors." And I called her many times, Chris. So people are accusing me of crime – this is disgusting, this make me sick. At one point those people will have to face what they did.

'So don't tell me that people are accusing me of having killed Peter, because we proved the contrary. Yes, he took too much Solpadeine, but he took too much alcohol also, and too much of everything. Did you know that they gave him paraceta-mol at the hospital? Peter was running a fever, he was sick, he had a bronchopneumopathy, he had many other problems, all his problems could have caused death. He was aware by leaving the hospital that he was in distress – they talked to him in Eng-lish, they wrote in English. Chris, I did all my best to help Peter, because I loved Peter.'

Realising that he had lost it for one brief moment, Despallières recovered his composure after a weekend in the country with his girlfriend and her son. Over the next few days our correspondence became less intense, less demanding, as he prepared for a court hearing towards the end of June at which his newly appointed barrister, Herzog, intended to apply for the murder charge to be thrown out: 'Everything is well prepared for the hearing on the 21st,' he wrote to me. 'I am more than confident . . . It should be the end of this terrible story.'

Nevertheless, in our correspondence he often went back to the accusation of murder, which still hovered over him. For example, in an email on 1 Jun, ten weeks after leaving prison, he wrote: 'About Peter, it has been proven five times now that he had many conditions and he is not dead because of paracetamol taken at one time. Peter was under many things since a long while. You have no idea what substances Peter was taking, the list is very long and he took all that shit for a [long time] because they can trace [it] in his hair almost all the substances Peter was taking . . . [The report is] oh so sad. I have all the reports from all the experts. I can give you copies of those, you will see how sad it is, and maybe you will understand how desperate I was. I loved Peter, Chris.'

By this time, he was repeatedly sending me 'evidence', which, to the untrained eye, might have proved his case. An attachment to one of his emails was the photocopy of a card, which had accompanied – in his words – 'a gift from my Peter'. In a large open scrawl, it read: 'Alex my darling, 20 years on you are still the love of my life. Always, Peter XXXX'. I ran it by four of the people who knew Ikin best and they all insisted it nowhere near resembled his 'awful scrawl', as one put it. I went back to Despallières: was this Peter Ikin's handwriting? As was often the case, he answered the question but went on to seal in it a diversion: 'Yes, the note is the treasure from my Peter. I am so happy to have found back those memories. They are important to my heart, more important than anything.'

Our correspondence took a particularly surreal turn when I wrote to him asking why more than one of his acquaintances testified that he had told them his real name was Yonan de Rothschild, a name his 'true family' – the Rothschilds – had apparently warned him not to use for fear of kidnap. I told him that Aurélien Beaucamp was just one who said he had told him that that was his real name. His reply was a little more than cryptic: 'About Aurélien, I don't know, he might have watched the TV and they said something like this. All I know is the people behind this horrible story are just some monsters, some clever ones because they met every single person and told them almost the same story. I received a message from Billy long ago, I was still in the UK, and he was telling me that he met all the people I might know. This is the starting point, since then people are making me look like the devil.

'My name is Despallières, and also I used Becker in the States. I am proud of who I am and I never told anyone that I was someone else. As you can see on the web, I use my real name, not another: my pictures are tagged Despallières, this is my name.'

To reinforce his argument to a doubting Clarisse that he used the name Becker legitimately, it later emerged that he had obliged her to watch the video Bilien had made of the adoption ceremony, already posted on Facebook.

For Despallières it was now a waiting game: waiting to have the charges against him dismissed while he anticipated a new life of freedom. He was, however, short on patience . . .

CHAPTER 20

ABSENT WITHOUT LEAVE

Things took yet another turn on 9 July 2011. I was driving into the Dorset town of Poole when I answered a call from a clearly distressed Clarisse: Alex had disappeared. It had been her birthday three days earlier and at around 7pm he had asked Noë to take his mother to a nearby park for an hour or so while he prepared 'a special surprise'. When they returned, Despallières had gone. He had taken only his mobile phone and a pair of pyjamas. He had no money and he had left behind an array of clothes Clarisse and her mother had bought for him. Calls to his phone went unanswered. Under the bed he had been sleeping on, he had left a stash of drugs, including the medication prescribed for his HIV condition.

Frantic with worry, Clarisse had telephoned every hospital in the surrounding area and finally the police, but the man who had become her close companion had disappeared. I did not share her feelings of anxiety: it was typical of Despallières when he decided to move on not to answer calls – at least not from anyone he knew. In the preceding fortnight, he had been working frantically on his computer. Unbeknown to Clarisse, he had given himself a new identity: he was now Alex Ando.

Though deeply upset that he had tricked her, during the following days Clarisse unburdened herself to me. She was particularly hurt that her son Noë – whom Despallières had gone to great lengths to bond with – was heartbroken by his disappearance, although he was still also fretting over the fate of his much-loved pet guinea pig. He had entered a room unexpectedly on one occasion to find Despallières feeding the animal something that looked like bread. When he asked him what he was doing, Despallières said, 'Shhhh, don't tell your mother.' Within hours, the precious pet became bloated, lost its hair and died.

Despallières had rarely eaten during his time with Clarisse and had stayed up most nights. The cause of his weight loss and increasingly nocturnal habits became clear when the medications he had left behind were examined: they included Modiodal, which suppresses appetite and is used by some as a cocaine substitute. One side effect is that the drug often causes mouth ulcers, giving users a symptom in common with AIDS sufferers. His stash also included cortisone, with which Clarisse was familiar since it had been prescribed for her ex-husband after he had undergone a heart transplant. The labels all bore the name of a pharmacy on the Rue Cardinet, which he had visited regularly.

Her desperate efforts to locate Despallières were largely stonewalled: his lawyer refused to speak to her on the grounds of 'client confidentiality', and when she attempted to place the medicines with him, the lawyer refused, so she took them to a storage depot in Montparnasse. The police were also unhelpful, pointing out that he was free to go wherever he wished until the end of the month when he was due to report to them under the terms of his bail condition. Once she had tired of leaving 'Alex, please call me' messages on his phone, Clarisse decided enough was enough and, fearful for her own and her son's safety, she changed the security pass on the front door to the building where she lived – even though at one point she had written to me: 'He is not dangerous to others, he is dangerous to himself.'

Despallières had proposed marriage to her during a prison visit earlier in the year, but she had turned him down, telling him, 'Marriage is not for me, Alex. I was in one marriage for ten years and it was shambolic. I don't like the official status of marriage. I am a free person and liberty is very important to me. I prefer just a dream.'

At this point she remained convinced that he was innocent of the heinous crimes he stood accused of, and believed, as did others, that the criminal accusations had been trumped up for some reason by Olivier Metzner: 'Of one thing I am certain,' she wrote to me, 'he is not a criminal. I loved Alexandre and I still love him. Even though our paths have separated, there will always be a place in my heart [for him] even though he makes me very sad. I want to take care of my history with him because there may be a bit of sincerity among his lies.'

There were numerous questions that required answers from her: had he given any indication before he left her that he was planning to do so? Had she spoken to Metzner, whom she had known long before she met Despallières? Had he been able to gain access to the money he had received in the settlement with Ikin's beneficiaries? Had he been in touch with either Bilien or Nail? Had she ever seen him buy Solpadeine? Alas, by now she was exhausted – too heavy of heart to answer any more questions: 'I am still under the influence of emotion,' she wrote in one particularly sad letter to me. 'I need time to understand.'

That, however, was to change. Clarisse left soon for a holiday in Spain with her son and parents. Our communications became spasmodic, but there was a dramatic development on 15 September which was to reignite our correspondence: Despallières had been found and re-arrested.

The story of his time on the run after he failed to honour his bail obligations proved to be as astonishing as the whole saga of events chronicled in this book. It is indeed a bizarre tale (and to protect identities, some names have been changed). After slipping out of Clarisse's flat, Despallières had gone to the Paris home of the kindly prison visitor Helene Clement – the apartment on the 17th arrondissement where I had first interviewed him. While he had been in prison, assured of his wealth, Mme Clement had loaned him €10,000, to make his incarceration 'more comfortable' ('That would have allowed him to buy plenty of drugs on the inside,' Clarisse was to say when we discussed the matter of that loan later).

Mme Clement and her husband owned a country house in Lisieux, a village in Normandy, close to a famous monastery.

The Clements took him there 'to get well'. As he was fed and pampered, Despallières assured his hostess that he would soon be able to repay the money he had borrowed from her in prison. Inevitably, however, he grew bored in the company of the septuagenarians and began taking walks into town. Finally, he decided to leave and, pausing only to gather his few belongings, left the house as surreptitiously as he had departed from the home of Clarisse, heading for the local station to catch a train back to Paris. By the time he reached the station, however, the last train had left and he checked into a hotel close by.

The hotel was owned by a woman called Delphine Emery, who happened to be a friend of Mme Clement. Delphine not only took him in, but she also quickly fell under the spell of her new guest and within days had dispensed with her long-term boyfriend 'to be with Alex'. 'Delphine's whole demeanour changed,' says one who witnessed a total transformation in her. 'Suddenly she would appear in the evenings wearing exotic cocktail dresses, seemingly in the hope of arousing Alex's interest.'

Mme Clement, meanwhile, was furious with Despallières's unannounced departure and, believing that Clarisse was still in touch with him, made repeated angry calls to her demanding to know his whereabouts. What's more, she said, she was going to sue him for the return of her €10,000 – if only she knew where to find him. Despite being a friend of Delphine Emery she seemed unaware that he was staying at her nearby hotel.

Delphine, meanwhile, had another friend she introduced Alex to, on 18 July 2011 – Genevieve Cadieu, a plump woman in her sixties. Seriously bothered by Delphine's attempts to seduce him, Despallières pleaded with Genevieve to 'get me out of here', so she took him to her nearby home. Not only did Genevieve also fall under his spell but so too did her sisters, Madeleine and Harriet. Growing more comfortable by the day in Genevieve's home, he regaled the three women with stories of his vast wealth and eventually persuaded Genevieve, along with Harriet and her partner, Christophe, to drive him to a small country town for the day. Once there, while Genevieve ran some errands, he told Harriet and Christophe that he was interested in buying 'a large property' in the area. They took him to an estate agent who had just such a property on the market but was unable to take them to see it without the permission of the owner, who was away. 'Never mind,' said Despallières. 'I will probably buy it and install you two as resident staff.' No one mentioned it to Genevieve until the estate agent subsequently called her number to say an appointment could now be made to view the house. The deception, small as it was, caused a deep rift between her and her sisters.

In fact, all three sisters quarrelled fiercely about Alex, and they became a divided family while he remained under Genevieve's roof. Things came to a head when Genevieve threw a dinner party in Despallières's honour, inviting her niece, Natalie Coutrot, and Natalie's boyfriend, Eric Point, to join them. At the table, Despallières began his now-familiar spiel about his wealth and 'incredible success', but it did not ring true to Point, who grew increasingly annoyed and suspicious. When he returned home later that night, Point looked up the stranger-from-nowhere on the internet, discovering as he did so that Despallières stood accused of at least one murder – that of Peter Ikin – and was being investigated in the matter of two other suspicious deaths, those of his parents. And that the Brigade Criminelle were anxious to get news of his whereabouts, since by now he had broken bail.

Local police were informed and, in a hurriedly prepared operation, they descended on Genevieve's house with guns drawn. A young neighbour who witnessed the assault says he thought they had come to arrest him over a stash of marijuana he kept for his personal use. Genevieve was not at home when the raiders arrived, so they kicked down the front door and barged in to execute their search warrant. Initially it appeared that the house was empty, but as they were about to leave one officer noticed a movement in a huge pile of clothing heaped on the kitchen floor. Beneath it they found Alexandre Despallières. Robbed of his dignity but offering no resistance, he was arrested and escorted back to Paris.

Back in the capital, Despallières was not returned to Fresnes for fear that he might encounter a drug baron who had entrusted him to take some money to another – money that perhaps had failed to arrive. So it was from the Maison d'Arrêt la Santé – the prison in which Bilien had been incarcerated for six months – that Alex wrote to me on 3 October, explaining that he was back in detention 'because I did not respect the one month control [bail stipulation]'.

Employing his usual cryptic terms, prisoner number 294411 went on to blame everything and everyone for his predicament: 'After eleven months in detention things are not that easy outside. I discovered more people who betrayed me; one of those was my brother, Marc. Then there were a few other things, so if you add all these things together, your head spins and you just run away because the pain was too high to handle. I got sick but it wasn't important.'

Of his latest incarceration, he was more upbeat: 'The police arrested me. But they were so nice with me, nothing to compare with the first time. I can say now there are some policemen who are very nice. The detention here [at la Santé] is much better also. Fresnes was hell, this jail is so different. The people who work here are polite; they treat you like a human being.'

He added a kindly and flattering comment: 'I respect you, Chris, because you search for the truth.' He was, of course, oblivious to the truth of others, which I had learned as I researched this book. It was a letter to me which he composed from his bunk in cell 231 on 17 October that produced a big surprise: 'What I have is a bomb,' he began. He claimed to have discovered that it was not his friend of more than two decades, Olivier Metzner, who was responsible for his incarceration, but his more recent lawyer, Thierry Herzog: 'When I was in Fresnes, I thought it was because of Olivier Metzner. But once free, I read all the press [reports] and started to understand. Olivier is not the one who wanted me in detention, but Thierry had a very good reason. The more the press was talking about me in a very disgusting way, the more the press explained that I shared my life with Olivier for years. So this was the best they could do to Olivier, to manipulate me, letting me think I was there [in prison] because of Olivier – and they could ask favours, they grabbed Olivier by the balls. Imagine [how] it looks for Olivier; like his friend for decades was a murderer. Well, it was very well done because they fooled me.'

Then came 'the bomb'. On his previous release on bail, he had gone to see Herzog and had secretly recorded the meeting. 'So, I go to Thierry's office. I play dumb as usual and I get all I needed in a memory card and I place some copies [with a] few friends, three of them, and now I feel much better. It is a very tricky situation; I was so fucked up so it is very soon time for me to correct everything. And since you are my friend and I trust you, I will make sure that a copy of the recording is addressed to you.'

He was proposing that I – the writer investigating the allegations against him of being a serial killer and a master fraudster – was to be the guardian of a recording he had made of an alleged conspiracy by his own (and the president's) legal representative. In the event the promised tape never was delivered, but he wrote to me again a week later (24 October) saying he was trying to get someone on the outside to send a copy to me. His next step, he declared, would be to sit down with Olivier 'to give him my side of the story . . . You know, Chris, they really fooled me well. All the time I was in Fresnes I thought it was because of Olivier. My attorney, Thierry, was coming to see me very often. How could I understand? There was no way for me to understand. I should have kept in my mind that Olivier had been a friend for decades, but in detention it is hard to focus properly.

'When I was arrested in Lisieux the police were very kind with me. I explained to them that I was used and still used for arrangement. They told me that made them sick because not only has justice been fooled but also the police itself has been taken for some kind of stupid people. The head of the police in this town even told me they hate to be manipulated. So I am not very scared of what is going to happen, because the truth is on its way, and also because I did nothing of what they accused me. My current lawyer is a nice lady, I am sick of those big lawyers. I know them very well and my last one was a real disaster!'

On 14 November, Despallières wrote to me: 'I am not looking forward to spending Christmas in prison – but it doesn't change a thing, this period of the year is not a good period for me. All I need is to work on getting better . . . I need to collect my mind, but I know it will take time.' He was especially enthusiastic about his new lawyer, Laure Heinich-Luijer – 'She is the perfect fit for me.' He had discovered Heinich-Luijer online, since she also wrote for a blog, www.Rue89.com.

He had, he went on, been able to persuade the new judge (with whom he appears to have established a mutual fondness) to allow him to cancel a meeting with her on the grounds that it had been scheduled for 12 November, which would have been the third anniversary of Peter Ikin's death.

Intent on winning back the friendship of Olivier Metzner, he had managed one small step towards his goal: 'Concerning Olivier, a few weeks ago I saw . . . a friend of Olivier and [me], another lawyer called Benoît Chabert,' he wrote to me. 'He kissed me and told me that Olivier knew I have been used by Herzog. Olivier and I – it is a long story, we have a long past together, so I am confident for after.'

The drama of what actually happened during his stay in Lisieux – and how he got there – was decidedly airbrushed in the account he offered me: 'Genevieve used to be a friend of Delphine for many years. Delphine is just nuts. Genevieve is just a big heart; I think she is terrific and adorable. Helene [Clement] used to visit me in Fresnes and when I got out she helped me in many ways – she is an angel. I owe her a lot. But when I discovered my brother Marc betrayed me my whole universe collapsed, [so] I decided to leave everything and everyone.

'You have to understand that my mind is not and wasn't working well. I have been depressed for a while now and all these people telling all these bad things about me doesn't help. Marc was the last person I let fool me. Since then, I haven't spoken to the ones around me. I know no one understands why I left [Paris] and why I stepped back from [everything] but deep inside me I sabotaged the little I had in order to make sure the [friends] I had wouldn't betray me. Now I know who my real friends are, and it is better that way. Sometimes when you get lost, you sometimes need to get more lost in order to find your way. I had to deal with so many things; I was lost so I let it go from everywhere.'

There was a sad element to the letter he wrote me from his new cell (he seemed rather pleased to have moved to cell 009 in Division 1) on 26 January 2012: 'I haven't been in touch with Clarisse and, as you pointed out, I owe her an apology. As I told you, I was very lost and I get scared to lose what I have left, so I run away. I think I needed to clean my head then I will have to clear my name – which is not an easy task after all the horrible things written by the press . . . I miss Clarisse so very much and I love her deeply. With time she might understand. At least I hope so. I felt the same for Noë, I love him. We were very close.

'Concerning Delphine from the hotel, she had a crush on me. She was nice at the beginning and then she became freaky; she wanted more from me, but I had nothing to offer her. It is Genevieve's sister who informed the police where I was, but honestly . . . it is better like this. I mean the only way to make this nightmare end is by facing the judge and I am confident enough to write that to you. The situation is going to [end] very soon . . .

'I did manage to contact Olivier: I sent him a letter for the New Year and I apologised to having trusted Thierry Herzog. But someone told me that [Olivier] knew I have been manipulated.'

Anxious as always to demonstrate that he was as interested in me and my work as I was in him and his story, he ended his letter with comments about the biography of Vladimir Putin I had just finished, writing: 'I am sure it is a great book and I cannot wait to read it.'

If Genevieve Cadieu thought she had seen the last of Despallières when he left her home under arrest, then she could not have been more wrong. The worst episodes of her life lay ahead.

On 14 February 2012 – Valentine's Day – he returned to Lisieux and her home. It was the day after his case had been heard at La Cour de Cassation, the highest court in the French judiciary system, which had ruled that on humanitarian grounds he should be remanded on bail instead of in custody.

The prison authorities had asked Genevieve if she would allow him to use her address for correspondence. She agreed but was surprised when he turned up on her doorstep expecting to be able to stay 'for a few nights'.

Taking pity on him because of his poor health, she agreed. After all, he would prove no trouble to her since he was (as she thought) gay and 'extremely charming'.

They spent long evenings in conversation and during one he told her he was jubilant that the court had decreed that the statement he had made to Philippe Meyer when he was arrested could not be used in evidence if and when he came to trial because he had been under duress and no solicitor had been with him at the time.

He went on to recount to her events in the run-up to Peter Ikin's death. He said that he had gone to a nightclub with friends, having hidden Ikin's teeth so he would not follow them, saying his partner was 'fat and ugly' and he was ashamed to be seen with him. He went on to pass similar remarks about his mother, adding that he regarded the well-preserved Marcelle Becker as his real mother: 'She is rich and beautiful.'

A few weeks later Despallières was joined at the Cadieu household by a 24-year-old Malaysian man, Yeoh Koh Seong, a fellow prisoner he had befriended in Maison d'Arrêt la Santé. The two were to stay rent-free for the best part of a year, during which, according to Genevieve's police statement, Alex stole money, a computer, mobile phones, identity papers and bank documents from their hostess, her sister Madeleine and two friends.

Mme Cadieu was obliged to pay €300 a month to keep them in the cigarettes the heavy smokers demanded (Despallières was a 60-a-day man). When she told them she was running into debt by meeting their demands, Despallières arranged for €8,000 to be sent to Koh Seong from his family in Malaysia via the local Western Union office. Because his passport had been confiscated, he did not have adequate means to prove his identity, so the money had to be sent in Mme Cadieu's name. Although she handed the cash over to him, he went on to later claim that she received it in 'payment' for the food and accommodation she provided for both men during their stay, when actually they paid her nothing.

When her funds had dried up, Genevieve – with a little encouragement from her guests – got a job as a cleaner, working at a mansion close to Deauville, which was occupied only at weekends. It was, in fact, a splendid residence owned by a wealthy Jewish businessman who, at his weekday apartment in Paris, happened one day to tune into a television programme, *Sept à huit*, in which he saw a man sat in his house, in his favourite armchair, being interviewed about accusations of murder levelled against him. Alexandre Despallières had persuaded Mme Cadieu to allow him to use the house for interviews, telling interviewers that it was his country residence.

But worse, Genevieve Cadieu was to tell police that the food Alex prepared for her was drugged. Treated like a maid in her own home, she was mostly required to cook their meals, but he regularly made what she described as 'strange-tasting soups' for her which he said were concocted from an eastern recipe.

Always an active woman, she would begin to feel faint after lunch, would fall into a deep sleep early in the evenings, and found it a struggle to get out of bed in the mornings, typically suffering a thumping headache. These were the same symptoms experienced by Peter Ikin, Despallières's parents and Marcelle Becker. When she said she needed to go to the hospital for tests after suffering unexplained falls, Despallières said there was no need, she should 'just go to sleep'. When she tried to insist, he told her not to go to the local hospital but that he would arrange for her to go to the best hospital in Paris, assuring her that he knew all the doctors.

Growing increasingly weaker, Genevieve found it impossible to counter the barrage of impositions by her so-called guests. Mme Cadieu put on 20 kilograms from the quantities of food they fed her, and the lack of exercise. Accordingly, there were few moments for laughter in the household, but Despallières did raise a smile from her pained face when he told her that, whenever he gave an interview, he stuffed a rolled-up face-cloth in his underpants to give the impression that he was well-endowed.

During his stay there, I wrote to Despallières to ask him which actor he would like to play him if this book were ever made into a film. It was a ruse on my part; I wanted to reignite our correspondence, which seemed for a while to have cooled. It seemed to put the thought into his head, however. He contacted one François Davoust, a financial advisor in Calvados, a region of Normandy noted for its apple brandy, saying he was going to be the subject of a Hollywood film and asking Davoust to be his agent.

They signed a contract and Despallières asked Davoust to drive him to Paris for a meeting with 'a movie producer'. Alas, it was no producer he was meeting, but the eminent writer Brad Stone, whom Despallières had convinced to write his *New York Times* exposure of Stickam back in 2007.

Stone takes up the story for a subsequent article published in *Bloomberg Businessweek*:

> Davoust dropped Despallières at the Bloomberg offices and waited in the lobby of a hotel across the street. Afterwards, Despallières said the project was

on track and promised to fly Davoust and his family
to California, where he had arranged a meeting
with Lady Gaga. Soon after, however, Davoust discovered that the SIM cards had been removed from
two of his cell phones, and that someone had used
them to make calls to Malaysia. Davoust tried to
reach Despallières in search of an explanation but
his calls weren't returned. He, too, filed a complaint
with the police. He has yet to meet Lady Gaga.

Genevieve Cadieu's nightmare was to end on 8 February 2013,
when Despallières announced that he had to go back to Paris for
a meeting with openly gay mayor Bertrand Delanoë, and he
would be taking Koh Seong with him. Genevieve took her two
lodgers to the station to catch the 13.26 train to the French capital, and that was the last she was to see of them for a long time.
Once they had gone, she began to recover from her malaise –
there was no more fainting, no more vertigo, no more falling
asleep unexpectedly, no more falls. Only when the mist had
lifted did she realise the full extent of her losses. She had incurred
substantial debts during Despallières and Koh Seong's stay. As a
result, her house was repossessed, obliging her to move into her
sister's home. At 61, she had lost everything she had ever worked
for. The local police were informed, and they submitted a
detailed report to those at the Brigade Criminelle who were
investigating Peter Ikin's death. Genevieve Cadieu's name was
duly added to the list of victims of crimes laid at Despallières's

door. When Mayor Delanoë was informed that his name had been used, he notified the Paris prosecutor to ensure he wasn't swept up in any intrigue.

Despallières remained at large using a huge fan base he had built on the internet to air all the wrongs he said had been done to him. 'If they find me guilty,' he said of the possibility of one day being brought to trial, 'I won't do 20 years in jail. I'm ill. They will have to release me. I'm sick.'

There is a sad postscript to this episode of the story. Despallières's wish to one day be reunited with his long-term friend Olivier Metzner was never to be granted. Less than six weeks after Despallières made his sudden departure from the home of Mme Cadieu, on 17 March 2013, the lawyer's body was found floating in the sea off Boëdic, the island in the Gulf of Morbihan he had bought for his retirement. Having miscalculated the tides, the corpse had not drifted out to sea as he had intended. Close to the body was his yacht, the fine vessel on which he had been planning to sail the world.

A police source close to the investigation confirmed that despite his plans, it was clear that Metzner had committed suicide.

Another said M. Metzner was being blackmailed by a former lover.

CHAPTER 21
THERE COMES A TIME . . .

Several dozen people turned up at the small restored chapel on the island of Boëdic to bid their final farewell to Despallières's long-term lover Olivier Metzner.

They formed a procession filing to the western end of the island to witness the scattering of the great man's ashes in the sea from a rock facing the setting sun – a spot he'd loved dearly.

At his home close to the shore, Metzner had left several letters in which he indicated his desire to end his life, together with a list of people to be notified of his passing. Methodical to the end, he'd even attached their telephone numbers. The letters he'd left led investigator Thierry Phelippeau to conclude that he'd committed suicide by drowning, a sad end to the 63-year-old's brilliant career. Was it a coincidence that Despallières had been nearby when his one-time benefactor had met his end?

In legal circles it was well known that Despallières and Metzner had fallen out. The relationship – both personal and professional – had ended acrimoniously. Metzner had sent Despallières a message which read, in effect, 'I'm withdrawing from your case. Find another lawyer.' It was no coincidence that Despallières had chosen Thierry Herzog to succeed Metzner as his legal representative. Metzner and Herzog were fierce professional rivals, having sat on opposite sides in the trial following the Clearstream affair, a political scandal in the run-up to the 2007 French presidential election.

To add to Metzner's embarrassment, his former lover had made an astonishing accusation to the police during the investigation into the fake Ikin will, that the drafting of it had been his — Metzner's — idea. His relationship with Despallières had been attracting unwelcome publicity at a critical time, since Metzner had been knee-deep in the Bettencourt case and had not needed the distraction that his beau was causing.

Significantly, Metzner did not leave a letter for his longtime intimate friend, Alexandre Despallières, the playboy gigolo he had courted for more than two decades. Surely it can have come as no surprise to Despallières. Metzner had refused to take calls from him once they had gone their separate ways.

It would not have escaped Despallières's attention that not only was there no farewell letter for him, but he was also excluded from the list of those Metzner had named in his will.

Instead, almost the entire fortune was left to a young lawyer Metzner had shown affection for — and that included his yacht, thought to be worth €4.5 million, and the island of Boëdic, which was worth twice that. Then there was the firm and its 17 highly qualified staff — but the name of the firm itself went to another of those in good standing in Metzner's circle.

Given his boundless sense of entitlement, Despallières doubtless felt usurped by the legatee. But it was clearly a will of revenge and Despallières was not the only one to suffer.

Sadly, the intended recipient of Metzner's largesse was not up to dealing with the complicated estate, and Metzner's family took it over. Having found no buyer for Boëdic, they subsequently sold it for less than half its value. Meanwhile, in Paris, the 'Metzner Associates' plaque was being unscrewed from the wall at 100 Rue de l'Université, the palatial building which housed the offices he had founded and built into what was widely reputed to be the best criminal practice in Paris.

For his part, Despallières realised that there was no way he could cash in on Metzner's death. Instead, he traded information, most of it false, about the lawyer and his contacts in the government.

But was it also possible that he had blackmailed his lover into committing suicide? Acknowledging his power, Despallières had once said, 'If I talk, Mr Metzner will have to shut down his firm and he will go to jail.'

• • •

With Metzner gone, Despallières was aware he would have to search for a replacement, and he found it in a relationship with one Xin Wei, the son of a modestly successful Chinese businessman, initially becoming the manager of his new partner's friend, a singer known as Chou.

The encounter with Xin was probably the most romantic in his life, and the feeling seems to have been mutual. Xin said of his new boyfriend: 'I have never known anyone who loves me as much as Alex does.'

Once in a civil partnership with Peter Ikin, once married to his ally Laetitia Nail, and briefly the adopted son of the wealthy American widow Marcelle Becker, Despallières married Xin and the pair moved to Torcy, a town of 22,000 people close to Disneyland, to the east of Paris. They wed in what Despallières described as a simple ceremony among friends. There were just five of them, but enough to fill a table afterwards in a nearby bistro, where they had a celebratory dinner – spoiled only by the excruciating stomachache and sickness suffered by one guest and the claims by another that she'd had all her money stolen.

Then Despallières launched a company called K3OPS, which, although they lived in a humble apartment, claimed to have offices in London, Paris and the Chinese city of Shenzhen. Despallières was the president and Xin Wei vice president. Its website declared 'At K3OPS we are proud and blessed to be part of the 3D printing revolution.' Perhaps somewhat ironically, the slogan of Despallières's new venture was 'Build the Impossible'.

Despallières was assisted in setting up the new operation by Rona Barcas, a bright executive with Marriott Hotels. After meeting Despallières in the hotel where she was working on an audit at the Disneyland Marriott, Ms Barcas became a friend and often visited the apartment where Despallières and his new part-ner had set up home. Alas, after eating one meal there, she was taken violently ill with suspected stomach poisoning. Following a spell in hospital she left France after calling her husband, who travelled from Holland to take her back to their home in the Hague. Later she returned to Paris for a four-hour interview with Commander Meyer, who added a copy of her statement to his Despallières file. A sample of her hair was taken for analysis to establish what she had consumed to cause her illness. The result was never made public.

Relentless in his bid to solve the mystery of how Peter Ikin had died, Commander Meyer travelled to Australia in the early months of 2014 to interview those who had been close to Peter Ikin and a woman who knew Alexandre Despallières well – Petra Campbell. Next, he petitioned a judge for authority to fly to America and question Marcelle Becker. In California, he also wanted to ask Jesse Morfin about the conversation he said he'd heard between the three accused before they had set out for Sydney, where Despallières, the billionaire from nowhere, would knock on Peter Ikin's door on that fateful day in 2008. Of Meyer's activities Despallières had no clue, and he continued to cement his business plans.

. . .

In search of new fortunes, Despallières and Wei moved to the South of France in 2015, where their lives took a series of bizarre turns. Living in a shabby apartment on takeaway meals, they attracted little attention from their neighbours on the Rue du Panier in Marseille, a city which Despallières knew well from visits with his late father. The few would-be investors who were contacted were shown photographs of Alexandre with former president Jacques Chirac, and with Elton John, taken during the Ikin era. Based on his ability to con others and Xin's technical knowledge, Despallières was able to convince those he hoped would part with their money that he was responsible for some high-flying scientific inventions. Those who did initially invest brought in others eager to get a share of the promised pie. Not all his escapades in the business of confidence trickery were successful, however – one of their key investors turned out to be a Chinese swindler wanted by Interpol.

Boasting about the success of their enterprise, they moved out of their humble accommodation and set off to more salubrious home and business locations on the Côte d'Azur.

Finding still more people keen to invest in a company that claimed to recover energy – and therefore marketing free electricity – was no great stretch for Despallières. 'K3OPS to release the first eco-friendly source of energy to power-supply all your electronic devices,' he bragged on Facebook. Being able to turn on a light bulb without any apparent means of supplying electricity to it gave him licence to claim that he was indeed the founder of a potential billion-dollar operation.

To those he met, Despallières told a tale of Chinese friends in high places. Some said he claimed his husband was a member of a Chinese royal family, although China has been a republic since 1912.

He occupied grand suites in fine hotels: that no one questioned his ability to pay the bill owed much to a suitcase the contents of which he showed to anyone they needed to impress. The case contained what appeared to be a fortune in bank notes. Staff at one such hotel were told that the pair were MIGs – Most Important Guests – and their every wish was to be granted. They held court in their palatial rooms where Xin Wei chewed on cigars. They did not dine in the restaurant but ordered extravagant meals from room service. Hotel managers were told that a forthcoming visit by Xin Wei's family would pay their wages for a year.

Suspicions were not aroused until the hotel's management heard that Despallières had been asking staff about the hotel's IT systems, including the confidential information they held about their clients' credit card details and passport information. Such information would have allowed him to rob them of considerable amounts. Things came to a head when one employee who had seen the money in the suitcase said he thought it was fake, and that the two men were probably worthless. His words did not fall on deaf ears. After a serious review of the situation, Despallières was summoned to the executive office and told that his presence in the hotel was no longer in its interests. He should leave immediately, and he did.

Despallières's dubious activities continued, though his spending had to be curtailed, obliging him to settle for somewhat less glamourous accommodation. But by stretching his enterprise's brand online he tempted more investors on board, particularly from China, so the money kept coming in.

However, he fell out with one of his backers and it became apparent that his life was in danger if he and Xin remained in the area. Relatively rich with the genuine money raised from would-be investors, they returned to Paris in 2017, and there Despallières discovered that, because of his high-profile social media presence, he was now regarded as a leading light in the green-tech revolution. To his surprise he was invited to a party in the gardens of President Macron's residence to celebrate the best of French tech entrepreneurs.

His new prosperity allowed him to move to a swish apartment in Paris, one wall of which he decorated with a signed photo of Billy Gaff's friend Britt Ekland. Ms Ekland had inscribed the picture with the words: 'For Alexandre, the most beautiful man in the world.'

After good fortune seemingly smiled on him again for a handful of years, Despallières was rocked by news that the Ikin murder charges had not gone away after all. Until now he had escaped any legal scrutiny on technicalities.

Commander Meyer and his team had concluded their investigations. They had built a profile of Despallières which was supported by forensic evidence, and they were now in a position to proceed to trial.

In addition to the lethal levels of paracetamol in Ikin's body at time of his death – the silent witness in Meyer's investigation – the toxicology analysis of his hair demonstrated that he had consumed a higher-than-normal quantity of para-cetamol (380ng/mg of hair) in the two months before he died, squarely in the timeframe that Despallières had lived with him in London. Despallières's assertion that Ikin had stored large quantities of Solpadeine – up to 800 tablets – under the sink in his London apartment was disputed by Christine Barry, Ikin's housekeeper of 14 years, who testified that she had never seen any evidence to support such a claim. What's more, the blood tests taken in the few hours between his final exit from hospital and the time of death showed his body had consumed even more of the drug.

Ikin's financial advisor, in his testimony to the investigators, had made it clear that it was Despallières who'd wanted Ikin to join him in Paris once he had concluded his business in Brussels. This contradicted Despallières's assertion that it was Ikin who'd insisted on them meeting in Paris, a meeting that was to prove fateful for the older man. This had helped to sway the investigators towards believing that Peter Ikin had neither committed suicide nor died of natural causes, but that he had probably died at the hand of another.

. . .

Having failed to use what he called 'the power of China' to extricate himself from the possible life sentence facing him, Despallières tried a new ruse – one that he had used more than once before: his health. He stopped taking the medicine prescribed to him for HIV and became seriously ill as a result. The ruse succeeded but it did nothing to change the judge's mind about proceeding with the trial. The Despallières I knew could never have intended the drama to go beyond the point of no return. After he became increasingly ill and suffered several complications, his critical condition became irreversible. He was totally incapacitated and relied on Xin and a medical team to keep him alive. His defence systems under par, he contracted Covid.

It came as no surprise to the few close to Despallières that his admission to the Bichat Hospital early in 2022 was to be his last. He died there on 26 January, another Covid statistic. Other than Xin there were few to mourn his passing. Although he left behind a trail of unanswered questions, he would never face a murder trial or be legally branded a 'killer'.

Billy Gaff said, 'Good riddance. He did not deserve the life he robbed others of.'

There were others, however, who refused to believe that he had even passed away . . .

CHAPTER 22

AND NOW THE END IS NEAR

The date of 13 June 2022 would have been a significant one in the diary of Alexandre Despallières had he lived to see it. For it marked the start of his scheduled trial for allegedly murdering Peter Ikin and various charges related to falsifying Ikin's will from which he had benefited so massively.

Alas, since he had died 138 days earlier at the Bichat Hospital in Paris (his body having been cremated at the Cimetière du Père Lachaise, just as Ikin's had), Despallières had escaped the full justice of the law and possibly life imprisonment – that being the likely sentence for murder. Indeed, the charge was serious enough to have brought the trial to the all-important Cour d'Assises, where trials are normally heard with a jury present (although would not be on this occasion).

Had he been there, Despallières might well have thought that the band of armed soldiers surrounding the court was a testament to his importance, but not so. The military were there to guard those involved in the nearby trial of the 20 Islamic terrorists involved in the Bataclan massacre, one of the worst peacetime attacks to take place in Europe.

Those who were present, however, included the two who had been arrested alongside him: Jérémy Bilien and Vincent Bray. Like Despallières, Bilien had initially been under formal investigation for murdering Ikin. The Cour d'appel de Paris decided in May 2020 that there was insufficient evidence to send Bilien and Bray to trial for murder. There was a moderate feeling of sympathy for Bilien since he made it known that his father was an alcoholic who had bullied him badly as a child.

It was a hot day and no one in the court could have felt that more than Mme Emmanuelle Bessone, the court's president, as she struggled into the heavy robes her status demanded she wear. Mme Bessone had expected to be presiding over a prestigious murder trial and it must have come as something of an anti-climax to her and the two judges who sat on either side of her, Claude Choquet and Arthur Courillon-Havy, to learn that the case before them was nowhere near as important as that of the Islamic terrorists. Not for her a courtroom with the comfort of air conditioning – something they had in the new courtroom next door, which had been specially built for the terrorism trial.

Nevertheless, the heat in the courtroom did nothing to lessen the stress generated by the occasion. The president of the court, Mme Bessone read out from the evidence that she was provided with that it was Bilien who had booked the hotel room in which Ikin was to die, and Bilien who had signed the hospital release forms which deprived the Australian of the medical care he'd so desperately needed – after all, the doctors had warned Bilien that if Ikin was taken from the hospital he was likely to die.

French law does not make it easy for evidence to be submitted or challenged. There is little cross-examination because the 'record' has already been assembled; witness testimony in general is limited and cross-examination even more so. If the judges decide to hear a witness they will generally ask the questions that they had in mind and then invite the parties to ask further questions. But this process is usually short. An attorney attempting to dominate a witness with US-style cross-examination will be cut off.

In the courtroom, Ikin's friend John Reid was sat just a few rows from the judges and the defendants. It was a testament to the tenacity of Reid and Gaff that two of the conspirators were even here standing trial, for that had looked only a distant hope when the case was initially closed in February 2009, following the autopsy that had found that Peter Ikin had died of heart failure and hepatitis.

Such detail in the courtroom would not have been looked upon kindly by the likes of John Reid, or by the elderly woman sat at Reid's side who was tightening her fist around a small bunch of papers – the prescriptions she had been obliged to take to her neighbourhood pharmacy on Despallières's behalf. For this was Genevieve Cadieu, the woman he had swindled out of everything she'd ever owned, including her home in Lisieux which she had welcomed him into.

Because no one was being tried for murder, the court was meeting in a reduced format: there was no jury present and the time allocated for the trial was reduced from two weeks to two days. The assembly included the lawyer for Ikin's family, Marion Gregoire, Solenn Le Tutour for Bilien, Petra Lalevic for Bray, and the prosecutor Jean-Christophe Muller. Seated behind them were three cheerleaders for the defendants – Bilien's mother, Nadia Muller, and sister, Amandine Bilien, and the man Despallières had most recently married – Xin Wei, also known as Guillaume Wei. Xin did not cut the figure of a successful scientist or businessman. He had written to me on one occasion to explain that he was a mathematician who was working on a project to help solve the world energy crisis. But in his long letter he'd done nothing to suggest that he was someone who had fallen for the wrong man. This poorly dressed, scrawny young man, who was obviously very nervous, could not have forgotten that he had once written to the court expressing the view that the prosecution of Despallières was politically motivated to sully Olivier Metzner's reputation, following the prosecution of President Sarkozy in the Bettencourt case.

The court heard that Bilien and Bray were both accused of fraud and forgery. Despallières would have been in the dock on the same charges. He'd attempted earlier to have these charges dismissed on the grounds of double jeopardy, meaning a person cannot be tried more than once for the same crime. However, since the current trial in France was a criminal case and the High Court action in London completed in December 2009 had been a civil case, his appeal had been unsuccessful.

The court president's opening statement took two hours to deliver but it is best summed up by her announcement: '*Alexandre Despallières, il est mort*.' Because he was dead, the case against him would not be heard.

There were murmurs in the courtroom. Should it not be known that just three days after Ikin's death Despallières had been searching the internet for a lawyer who dealt with wills? Or that the items found by the police in the tin box he'd kept in his lock-up in Paris included a letter he had received from his solicitors informing him that under Australian law his civil partnership with Peter was unenforceable, making it clear that he was not a legal beneficiary of Ikin's estate?

Yet from statements provided to the police and from records obtained from Despallières's computer, it was clear that in order to inherit, Despallières had crafted the last will and testament of Peter Ikin on his computer and had dated it 7 August 2008 – a date he had picked because it was one on which it could be proved that Ikin was in the French capital. Bilien had then perfected the forgery by copy-and-pasting Ikin's signature, obtained from another document, and had then photocopied the fake will several times in a bid to remove any hint of the origin of the signature. To perfect the aged look of the document it had then been placed on a radiator and under a sun lamp. Despallières had claimed during the investigation that the idea of creating a fake will had been Olivier Metzner's, a claim emphatically denied by the latter before his death. Perhaps if the legal eagle had had any part in the drafting of the fake it would not have been 'really shitty', as Despallières himself described it.

Bilien took this document to Paris in January 2009, where he met Vincent Bray at a McDonald's in the Gare du Nord, to witness the multimillion-dollar fake will as they munched cheeseburgers. Bray had admitted that the fake will bore his signature.

The court heard that for his part Vincent Bray had tested the patience of the investigators by declaring that when he had added his signature to the fake will, he had not understood English and had been unaware that the document Bilien was asking him to sign was a will – and one that Paul Smith had already refused to sign. The court gave little credence to his explanation since the word 'TESTAMENT' was clearly written in capitals on the document he signed, and the French word for 'testament' is *testament*. In any event, the document he was asked to witness bore Ikin's name – a man he had never met. Moreover, it was back-dated by some months, and he himself back-dated his signature, as if he had witnessed the fake will months earlier.

His co-defendant, Bilien, said that he had explained to Bray that the document was a will and it was to replace the one that had allegedly been stolen in a burglary at Ikin's home in London.

Having both signed it they left the burger bar, and Bilien wasted no time in faxing it to Despallières's English solicitor to enable Despallières to make the claim on Peter Ikin's estate as his sole heir. Many were incredulous that an English court had granted probate on a photocopy of a will pertaining to Ikin, even though he was not domiciled in England but in his homeland, Australia. But that was down to Despallières, and he was dead.

Police chief Philippe Meyer could have been forgiven the smug smile that crossed his face when he heard how the diligence of his detectives had uncovered Despallières's ruse to give the two defendants a cover story about their fake meeting with Ikin in Paris. Despallières had even written a script for them to follow, and then had sent them to the upmarket Ladurée tearoom to rehearse their story. There they picked out a table they were to say that they had sat at, and ordered hot chocolate and macarons, just as Despallières's script dictated. This was in the event that they were called as witnesses in the High Court hearing against him, to provide authenticity for the 'fake will' in his defence.

Bray had duly been brought to London to falsely certify, in the presence of a notary, that he had witnessed the fake Ikin will on 7 August 2008.

Freed of all speculation, Despallières had filed for probate on Ikin's estate on 27 February 2009, 107 days after the record industry maestro's death. Once probate was settled he set about enjoying his ill-gotten gains.

One of the first to benefit had been Vincent Bray, to whose HSBC account he had transferred £10,000, which Bray had later claimed was to make up for lost earnings as he had been obliged to resign from his job in Paris and go to London to be with Despallières. Despallières had also given him a Porsche, which he had driven once but, fearful of its power, had given back.

Bilien sipped from his water glass as he listened to Bessone's opening statement and evidence provided by Commander Meyer. Yes, it was he who had rented the rooms in the Abba Montparnasse Hotel, and he who had signed the hospital release for Ikin, despite knowing that Ikin was acutely ill. As Ikin's husband, Despallières had been his next of kin and he should have been the signatory. When asked by the prosecution lawyer why he hadn't gone back to check on Ikin in the hotel room, he shrugged his shoulders and said he didn't know.

Bilien and Despallières had been companions for ten years after meeting on a dating website. That was until their arrest in June 2010. As part of his defence, Bilien would say that Despallières had had a power over him that had amounted to psychological control, and that he had been violent to him. Doing everything Despallières had instructed, he had had very little contact with his family since meeting him, and it was only after he was charged in 2010 that he had fully reconnected with his mother and his sister. According to his lawyer, Bilien's only crime was 'to be devoted to Alex'.

Had Despallières been on trial, how destructive it would have been to his defence to hear about the bizarre game he had initiated during a visit to the home in La Ferté-Bernard of Harriet Cadieu's partner, Christophe. It had been a late August evening in 2011 and Despallières had been there following a dispute with Delphine Emery which had obliged him to make a hasty departure from her hotel.

Host Christophe had said he'd noticed that Despallières had seemed stressed when a police vehicle had passed by outside, and his visitor had explained it away by boasting that he had powerful enemies. He had, he'd said, once been imprisoned for daring to criticise the policies of President Sarkozy, who even wanted to kill him.

Christophe had said he was impressed on this occasion by Despallières's knowledge of pharmacology, but surprised when the visitor had suggested 'the game': a challenge in which each of them was to suggest what they thought was the best way to kill someone. Helpful as ever, Alex had offered a choice between choking, hanging, stabbing and poisoning. Despallières himself had opted for drug poisoning, declaring that 'one could go to the end without it being proven' and that 'there were not necessarily any traces left . . .'

According to the toxicology report (and confirmed by the court's appointed medical expert, Dr Lecomte) there had, however, been traces left in Ikin's blood and preserved organs of a lethal level of paracetamol in his body, and it was that that had killed him. But, as Mme Bessone had decreed, Despallières was dead and therefore could not be presumed guilty as there had been no trial.

The evening at Christophe's home had certainly helped the police in finding their man. They were acting on a complaint by Harriet Cadieu, Genevieve Cadieu's sister and Christophe's partner, that during his visit Despallières had stolen items from Christophe's home and that he was 'a Machiavellian, manipulative, lying character playing a double game with everyone'.

It would also have come as a crushing blow to Despallières to be publicly exposed as penniless in a court of law. A psychiatrist called to analyse him said he'd displayed characteristics of a narcissistic personality. So, when he'd turned up unannounced at Ikin's apartment and declared, 'I am rich, I'm dying and I love you,' he was describing a fantasy world that supported his delusion of grandeur and his ability to exploit another human without guilt or shame.

Finally, the question as to whether Despallières had terminal tumours was laid to rest by a medical team appointed by the court. Yes, he was HIV positive – he had described himself as living with the sword of Damocles over his head, having been diagnosed with HIV in 1985 – but no, the medical team pronounced that he did not have the terminal tumours he'd told Ikin he was undergoing treatment for in Mexico in the summer of 2008 at Carlos Slim's expense. Bizarrely, to fool Ikin as to his whereabouts, Despallières had been in Paris before moving to Guildford, England, with Meg Sanders, aka Sandrine Gaillot but properly known as Laetitia Nail. He'd claimed that the story of him having terminal tumours had been invented by Ikin simply because he had not wanted his friends to know that Despallières was HIV positive.

And there was shock in the courtroom when it came to light that among the items Despallières kept in his tin box stored at his lock-up was the photograph of Peter Ikin in his coffin with a smiling Despallières looking over him giving a thumbs-up. Meyer was clearly proud that his officers had discovered this piece of evidence.

In courtroom chatter, much was made of the fact that Despallières had not identified himself as Ikin's husband at the various hospitals to which he'd taken him in the days before his death. Instead, he'd said he was Peter's son, and even on the day of Ikin's death Despallières had offered his own liver for a transplant.

Few eyebrows were raised, then, when the prosecutor described Despallières, Bilien and Bray as 'the psycho, the manipulator and the idiot'.

At the Cour d'Assises, the laborious and meticulous investigation was finally concluding. It had spanned 12 years and three continents, and had challenged the minds of four different investigating judges. It was early afternoon on 14 June 2022, the second day of the trial, when the judges retired to consider their verdict. The two defendants faced a maximum sentence of three years in prison and a fine of €45,000. The prosecutor had asked the judges to send Bilien to prison for three years (less 30 months suspended) and hand down a two-year suspended sentence to Bray.

Some present were puzzled that the judges took three and a half hours to reach their conclusions, as it had been perceived as an open-and-shut case. When the court president finally delivered the verdicts, both men were found guilty as charged. Bilien was sentenced to 24 months in prison, including 18 months suspended. He was told he could leave the court and not go to jail as he had already served six months following his arrest in June 2010. He was also fined €5,000. Bray got a 12-month suspended sentence for forgery and complicity in its use, and a €2,000 fine.

At least none of those involved in this unsaintly mess were going to profit from their crimes. A joint bank account bearing the names of Despallières and Bilien and holding €606,201 was confiscated as an additional penalty. That was the money awarded to Despallières by the High Court in London in 2009 when it had judged in favour of the beneficiaries of Ikin's genuine will.

The reprimands meant little to those who had loved and lost a dear friend: Billy Gaff had said, 'Peter was my dearest and closest friend, a brother and so often a nagging mother! I miss him.'

At one point during our many conversations, Despallières asked me an unexpected question: 'Chris, I know a straight man who has a problem. He's fallen in love with a woman who isn't in love with him and she's giving him a hard time. It's wrecking his life. What should he do?'

By way of reply I quoted him some words I'd first heard many years previously: 'Tell him to ask himself, "Do I love her enough to leave her alone?"'

'Good enough for a song title,' he mused, smiling. 'Do I like them enough to let them live?'

And that was as close to a confession as I was ever going to get from Alexandre Despallières.

EPILOGUE

According to the Merriam-Webster dictionary, a psychopath is 'a person having an egocentric and antisocial personality marked by a lack of remorse for one's actions, an absence of empathy for others, and often criminal tendencies'.

All of this strikes a chord when it comes to Despallières. Charming, easily bored, lacking long-term ambition, a misplaced superiority complex, unpredictable, reckless and promiscuous – all hallmarks of psychopathic behaviour. Was he a Ted Bundy or Jeffrey Dahmer in the making, a Charles Manson without the facial hair? Had I risked my life by taking coffee with Despallières? Had he merely reined in his remorseless disposition on those occasions?

Like everything else about Despallières, it pays to dig a little deeper. Throughout our correspondence and interviews I did not get the impression of a man who was an all-out killer – although of course I might have been blind-sided by his charm.

But perhaps his condition better fits the symptoms of anti-social personality disorder, primarily behaviour that conflicts with social norms. I'm no expert, but listening to those that are, seven key symptoms have been nailed:

- A disregard for the safety of themselves and others
- Failure to follow the law
- Impulsiveness
- Irritability and aggression
- Lack of remorse
- Lying or manipulating others for profit or amusement
- A behavioural pattern of irresponsibility

Significantly, people with ASPD often begin to display signs of it before they reach the age of 15.

Despallières was a man of dangerous charisma, who skewed the dynamics of any group and could bend the will of friends – or were they followers? – to his own. Normally, I'd prefer that Peter Ikin's words were the last to appear in this account, as he is the man we don't want to lose sight of here, out of respect for all he achieved, all he suffered, and for the friends he left behind. As his good friend Peter Rix put it: 'We are all richer for his friendship and so much poorer without him. They just don't make many people like our PI . . .'

But on this occasion, the final segment of text belongs to Despallières, aged 45, who uploaded these words on the internet on 2 June 2013. Although that post has since disappeared, the polemic offers extraordinary insight into a man who was so adroitly fitted to the Oscar Wilde quote 'To love oneself is the beginning of a lifelong romance.' It might have been intended as innocently humourous and self-deprecating, but it also could represent something far more sinister. Following Despallières's death, the circumstances of how and why it was written will remain forever unknown.

Another Sunday on Earth, just like another one . . .

Hello out there, whoever is looking at me, including me (because I am probably looking at me too). I am glad someone else other than myself is looking at me. My name is Alex and I just wanted to share a few precious moments of my day-to-day life with you.

I lived in Los Angeles where everybody is fake. One night, when I kissed somebody at a bar, it was the weirdest kiss I have ever had; later on someone explained that it felt weird because the lips were fake. It is very hard for me to fit in, because I am so real from head to toe.

I worked in the entertainment industry where the fake is extremely fake and where I am extremely me, picture-perfect every single moment. It's hard work, but someone has to do it, and there is no one better than me, especially with all the practice I do to make sure that it is the case. Anyway, I think I fitted in perfectly, I brought that *je ne sais quoi* that LA lacks. I really don't get why people hate me because I am naturally beautiful, a lot of them pay mega bucks to become as beautiful as I am. My beauty was free so they should admire me.

I am so pretty that I just got beauty insurance for every inch of my body. Very few people have beauty insurance, it usually only covers a certain part of the body, but when you are [pretty] everywhere, you have to buy the whole package. To my knowledge, I am one of the very few persons so good-looking that I need the 100% coverage. The thing that sucks is that my deductible is half a million dollars. The only reason I got the coverage is because my beauty is all real and natural. If you've had any work done then you are not eligible for this type of coverage. If there is anybody else out there with the same coverage I would really like to meet them but I know that it is probably nothing more than wishful thinking.

Occasionally when I walk past storefronts I'll see somebody absolutely smashing out of the corner of my eye. Of course, I give attitude, but then I realise that it is my own reflection. However, even before I realise this, I have already hit redial for my attorney so I can file a lawsuit because I am kind of jealous and, as

I should know, there is nobody as cute as me. Seriously, it does happen: I really do get jealous of myself and, if I could, I would sue me.

At the office I pretend that I am working, but in fact I am scribbling on pieces of paper (I like drawing pictures of myself). I have approximately 5,000 drawings of me. I never realised that I could have so many drop-dead beautiful expressions. If you know anybody interested these drawings are for sale; I would sell them for $1,000 each. Truth be told I might be jealous of myself but I am also very generous: I have just given 8 of my auto-portraits as birthday gifts; the recipients were so happy to receive them. I love to touch people's hearts, I am like that, that's what gifts are all about. I wish I had more time to do what I really love which is write down whatever comes into my mind and create a story where I am always the hero.

Anyway, I figured it was time to make the leap into the next frontier, sharing my likes and dislikes; one of the things I really like is me and I know for a fact so does everybody who meets me.

I really hope you liked the beginning of my story and hope you don't hate me because I am beautiful. I used to beat myself up about it, and then I woke up and realised how fortunate I am. Everybody should love me for I am the chosen one, he who shall forever be beautiful and unpretentious. If everybody lived in my world there wouldn't be such a thing as jealousy and envy and there would be no need for democracy.

All my friends say that I am a very wise person. Let's face it, I am the wisest of all my friends and business associates. This is very difficult and tiring for me as people always come to me for advice and guidance 24/7. I understand them doing that, but it takes up so much of my time. So, finally I gave in and three months ago I started writing the new bible. It is long past due. I figure if people come to me, take my word as gospel and worship me I might as well have a book to back me up.

I am now on page 7,264 and I am at the part where everybody wants to be in my presence. There are only 24 hours in a day and people come from all over the world because the word is out that I can guide people to a better life. So I have slowed down some in my writing. I mean I have an average of 40 reservations a day of people wanting to see me. I am at the point where I might start charging, but I am still talking with my publicist trying to come up with a fair rate. My idea is $150 per 5 minutes. If they want a photo of me then it will cost them an extra $399.99 and if they want a photo with me then I guess it would cost $500 and an extra $250 for my (stamped) autograph.

My book will probably retail at $99.95 without photos – the one with my detachable photo to carry around with you always will retail for $149.95. There is also a statue of me being designed for your home. It will hold one candle so that when you are feeling down you can light the candle and pray to me (you do realise that of course the statue and candle will be sold separately).

Thank God – or is it me? – that I am not pretentious.

I could have been nominated for president on numerous occasions. I would do it really, but with my extremely busy schedule it just is not possible. There's no way for me to squeeze it in my agenda and, besides, the people need me; it is [true] I am more booked up than the president! Besides, I make more money than him from my drawings and don't forget the forthcoming sales of my book. Not to mention the statue . . . Also, since I already can't go anywhere without being mobbed by crowds, my security detail is larger than the president's and I have been on the cover of every magazine at least five times worldwide . . . Anyway, why would I want to be president when he is calling me for guidance?

Like I said, thank God that I am not pretentious. Some people think I am, but I know for a fact that I am not. I just don't understand how those people can pass judgement on me simply because I wear designer clothes, am to die for and absolutely refuse to talk to ugly people. I am 100% not pretentious, I really truly drive a 1978 Pinto – the license plate reads 'GOD IS HERE'.

In the part of town I call home everybody is wealthy, but they don't take care of themselves so you'd never know it – I really stand out there. I stand out not only because of my natural beauty but also because I am so humble about it. Because dealing with other people's reaction to even just a glimpse of me is difficult enough as it is I try and not draw too much attention to myself, but it doesn't work. I just shine and sparkle and always become the focus of attention and jealousies. For example, and as unbelievable as it seems, my beat-up 1978 Pinto was recently keyed – as if trying to punish the poor car for having such a fabulously gorgeous owner.

When at home I like to be naked and free – why should I cover such perfection from myself? The only problem is when I forget to draw the curtains there is a crowd outside before you know it. Some people have even moved into the neighborhood just to meet me. I am starting to get scared because I have no privacy whatsoever. Forget shopping on my own, I hire shoppers. And don't even ask about the postman . . .

I love to sleep as much as possible, that's how I stay so pretty, just like Sleeping Beauty. I prefer baths to showers, 'cause when I am lying there with my eyes closed, I can open them and always have a nice surprise: my reflection staring back at me from any one of the 27 mirrors in my bathroom. I've been told I look good from any angle and I wonder why people would think that shouldn't be the case, especially after all my practising in front of my mirrors. I hope I don't sound too much like 'I love myself', but I have to or nobody else will.

It is really hard to be me, you see, because everybody wants something. A date, my phone number, my picture, a piece of my clothes, the glass I drank from . . . Thank goodness I recently hired even more security guards. I am so afraid of being stalked, I am certain that it will happen to me. My email is being stalked because my photo was online. I had to take my photo off of my resume because I have so many job offers, and I saw my resume photo in ads that I knew nothing about. I sued that company but am certain that my picture is being used inappropriately without my permission all over the world.

When walking in crowds, people have this annoying habit of stopping right in front of me with this look in their eyes; they don't move out of my way, just stand there struck dumb, so I very slightly push them and say, 'Excuse me, model coming through.' This has worked pretty well so far. Being beautiful is really not easy. I mean I get bruises anytime I go out from people pinching my butt, my crotch, my chest and I can never catch who does it. So now my friends come along with a video camera. This tape is now my evidence to sue anybody who touches me.

I went to a new bar opening last night; it was the grand opening. I went and searched for a friend. When I arrived at 10pm everybody was a '2' and by 2am I was drunk and everybody was a '10'. Thank goodness I have a cardinal rule not to talk to people after 11pm because liquor impairs our thinking. When

I left and got back to my car there were three people trying to pick me up and there were seven notes on my windshield. I always give that kind of note to other people because you never know, it could be a match made in heaven. I would never call a number left on my car, especially since in the last few years I have gone out there has been not a single person good enough or even pretty enough for me to speak to.

If only more people thought like me, the world would be such a happier place.

I have to say that I do have one close friend, Tom, Tommy or is it Thomas, I don't remember his name exactly. He is extremely good-looking, but very, very poor and has no taste whatsoever. He is about the same size as me, without my definition. He is also very nice but not as personable as me. When he gets ready in the morning he takes over one and a half hours, whereas it only takes me ten minutes to be positively flawless.

When we go out I really do feel sorry for him because so many people are looking at me, trying to talk to me, asking me out. For every 25 people that come up to, one might say 'hi' to him. So I guess he is a good friend if he is still coming around with all my popularity, unless he is trying to be me (which happens very frequently). But only time will tell! I just wish on one level that he'll be able to keep up with the Joneses but I don't think it'll happen. I mean, it has never been possible for anybody to be as great as me on any level in the past. I really do like him, but I also believe he is trying to live in my world; and, as everybody knows, it is so impossible. On another level, just the thought of him believing that because I was nice enough to let him come into my life he can fit in my world makes me very angry because it is not realistic for poor people to even think that they could fit into my world.

My world is built on rich and beautiful, not poor and ugly. If you are poor or ugly, it is the same and it is not my world. But I guess that is what I deserve for bringing those types of people in my life as they are either freeloaders, gold-diggers or social climbers. So I think from now on I will ignore poor or ugly people – not that I ever really talked with any of them.

People really need to realise that I have a very sensitive body. I have allergic reactions to polyester, cheap soap and cologne. I can be sick for days. That is what separates the poor from the rich, I can always tell. Even my clothes are sensitive. If somebody even bounces off me then it leaves a fuzz ball. I really never understood how the low-income can never smell the odour they give off. Tom is all of that, trust me I know; by being his friend I spend a fortune on allergy medicine. So, regardless of how you look at this, it costs a lot of money one way or another when you bring trailer-trash friends into your life. I don't know how much longer I will be able to be his friend and since I am such a nice person and so down to earth I really don't know how I would be able to tell him, 'See ya, wouldn't want to be ya!' His family and friends will be devastated that he has lost the one and only rich flawless person he will ever meet in his life.

Speaking of his family, his mother is so ugly that when I ask her to go somewhere with me, like a restaurant, I make her sit in a corner, facing the wall. She is very nice, but so ugly that if I were to invest money into plastic surgery for her to become even presentable it would cost at least 3 million. So it is really necessary to weigh the pros and cons: I mean, do I like her enough to make that kind of investment.

She is really nice but so extraordinarily gross and the aroma that wafts out from her is enough to make you puke. I mean when I see her I need to take along my nausea pills. Thank God for those. For the first time in my life I have met someone whose breath smells like she ate fresh shit. I guess that is why I like to go eat with her; because I know that my appetite will be non-existent and so I will never gain weight. The first few times I had a meal with her, I sent my food back because I thought that's where the smell was coming from, but in fact it was her breath oozing across the table. I also don't like to sit with her too long because when she gets up a 'poof' of rotten ass comes from her seat. I am not sure what it is, but I have really almost thrown up every time I see her. I continue seeing her because she is so nice. She is much nicer than her son and she seems to be very real. If I ever do invest the 3 million dollars it will not fix the aroma problem. Her house smells so bad I am surprised that it is still standing. I don't know why I am calling it a house, it has wheels on the bottom and all the outside walls are tin. I guess they call that a trailer or something. Every time she gets a notice from the Health Department she just rolls it over to a new address. Since I have known her she has had 6 different addresses. I don't know if they have yard sales, but every time I go there, there are soiled wet clothes hanging outside on a cord. Do people really buy that? There is a sofa on the porch outside, I guess so she can guard the clothes.

When I listen to what she has to say, she mentions stores I have never heard of, like Kmart, Ross, Marshalls (do cops work there?). She talks about how fabulous those stores are but I have truly never heard of them. I think she is a pathological liar, but she is nice. For my birthday she made me a cake and it looked like dog food. So when I was leaving her neighbourhood I gave it to a bum on the corner. I think it was her ex-husband. I could swear I have seen him before in a photo with her and he was eating a piece of cake with his hands. When I gave the cake to the bum he started in on it right away and said it tasted familiar. That's when I put two and two together. I mean I recognised him, and he really is nobody I would know. I don't understand how their son ended up good-looking because his parents are dog-butt ugly. I know he'll age very fast because he'll never be able to afford a good face cream. I am sure his hair will fall out from cheap shampoo. I used to feel sorry for people like him, but have discovered that whenever you help them once then they expect your help forever. As you know, you cannot help people that don't help themselves, I call them parasites.

I am really looking to find a friend that is on the same level as me, but I know that it is just wishful thinking. I get sad sometimes knowing that there are so many trashy people and all I want is just one friend. It seems possible but the reality of it is not.

For those of you who may meet me, please do not get too close to me. I really do have sensitive skin as I already explained. Also, just so you know, even my friend Tom, or whatever his name is . . . When I go places with him I try to stay 15 feet in front because I am embarrassed to be seen in public with someone like him.

Nonetheless, if you ask, I will give you a catalogue of the parts of my life that are for sale. Once that is done, please walk away as soon as possible, I don't want to be seen talking to those of you who should, and no doubt will, pay me for my advice.

If we ever cross paths (and you're pretty enough) I will offer you words of wisdom, and when you get home you can tell your friends and family that God has spoken to you.

By: Alexandre Despallières

Alexandre Despallières with Billy Gaff

Peter Ikin and Alexandre Despallières in happier times

Despallières with Mirella Iacurci at Carr Hall Castle

Ikin and Despallières on their wedding day

Despallières with lawyer Olivier Metzner

Despallières with President Chirac

Miriam Gaff with
Despallières and his
cat, Ratatouille

Record mogul
Peter Ikin, before
he fell victim to
Despallières

THANKS . . .

. . . for their memories. Without the help of so many people who gave their time and information so generously to unfold this complex story, this book would not have seen the light of day. Clearly high up on my list of those who cooperated with me were John Reid and the much-missed Billy Gaff. Between them these two gave to me much of what they gave to their superstar charges, Sir Elton John and Sir Rod Stewart. Then there are the ladies – my wife, Gerri Hutchins, and Mary Jarrett, whose work and support helped enormously. Many of the people in the book are named for few requested anonymity, which says much about Peter Ikin. Others include the esteemed French journalist Chris Laffaille, *New York Times* writer Brad Stone and a number of Ikin's close circle of friends in Australia, including Brian Flaherty and Dolly East. To Peter's friend Roger Desmarchelier. To the informative Petra Campbell and to Mirella Iacurci. The helpful Commandant de Police at the Brigade Criminelle, Philippe Meyer, the distinguished French lawyer, Marion Gregoire, the ever helpful Miriam Gaff, and the hugely interesting American socialite Mrs Marcelle Becker.

Then there are my new friends at Ebury, Lorna Russell and Michelle Warner, who join forces with the good guys listed above.

Reading the manuscript leaves me with even fonder memories of the loyal and gifted Peter Ikin.

Photos provided by the following:

Images 1 and 7: Billy Gaff
Image 2: Dolly East
Image 3: Mirella Iacurci
Image 4: Dolly East
Images 5 and 6: Alexandre Despallières
Image 8: Robert Rosen